Two-Hour Appliqué

Two-Hour Appliqué

Over 200 original designs

Leslie Allen

Sterling Publishing Co., Inc. New York
A Sterling/Chapelle Book

For Chapelle Ltd.

Owner: Jo Packham

Editor: Amanda Beth McPeck

Staff: Malissa Boatwright, Sara Casperson, Rebecca Christensen, Amber Hansen, Holly Hollingsworth, Susan Jorgensen, Susan Laws, Barbara Milburn, Leslie Ridenour, Cindy Rooks, Cindy Stoeckl, Ryanne Webster, and Nancy Whitley.

Designers: Linda Durbano, Sharon Ganske, Holly Fuller, Amber Hansen, Mary Jo Hiney, Kristin Kapp, Phillip Romero, Cindy Rooks, and Alison Timothy.

Photography: Kevin Dilley for Hazen Photography

Photography Styling: Susan Laws

If you have any questions or comments or would like information on specialty products featured in this book, please contact:

Chapelle Ltd., Inc.
PO Box 9252
Ogden, UT 84409
(801) 621-2777
(801) 621-2788 (fax)

Library of Congress Cataloging-in-Publication Data

Allen, Leslie.
  Two-hour appliqué : over 200 original designs / Leslie
  Allen.
    p. cm.
  "A Sterling Chapelle book."
  Includes index.
  ISBN 0-8069-4277-0
    1. Appliqué - - Patterns.   I. Title
TT779.A42   1996
746.55'5 - - dc20   95-49198
                                                          CIP

10 9 8 7 6 5 4 3 2

Published by Sterling Publishing Company, Inc.
387 Park Avenue South, New York, N.Y. 10016
© 1996 by Chapelle Limited
Distributed in Canada by Sterling Publishing
c/o Canadian Manda Group
One Atlantic Avenue, Suite 105
Toronto, Ontario, Canada M6K 3E7
Distributed in Great Britain and Europe by Cassell PLC
Wellington House, 125 Strand
London WC2R 0BB, England
Distributed in Australia by Capricorn Link (Australia) Pty Ltd.
P.O. Box 6651, Baulkham Hills
Business Centre, NSW 2153, Australia
Printed and Bound in the United States

Sterling ISBN 0-8069-4277-0

1

This chapter is your handbook to appliqué. There are step-by-step instructions for many appliqué techniques, common embroidery stitches, dimensional ribbon work and painting techniques.

• Welcome to Two-Hour Appliqué •

• How to Use This Book •

This book is divided into three chapters. Before each chapter is a chapter table of contents.

Chapter 1 contains the general instructions. The first section of Chapter 1 describes the appliqué process from beginning to end. The next section contains step-by-step instructions and photos illustrating several different appliqué techniques. Following is a section containing step-by-step instructions and illustrations for several embroidery stitches and dimensional ribbon work used with the appliqué.

Chapters 2 and 3 are projects and patterns chapters. Each chapter is divided into sections containing a photograph of a finished project or projects followed by patterns for that project plus additional designs. The additional designs can be finished in the same way that the photographed pieces were finished. For instance, the first section of Chapter 2 begins with a photograph of four framed birdhouses. The additional designs can also be framed and hung together as a set. However, the finished pieces are meant only as ideas—every design can be finished in many ways.

Traditional appliqué designs and techniques are found in Chapter 2. Traditional appliqué includes all of the basic appliqué techniques.

Chapter 3 is contemporary appliqué. This chapter covers a broad spectrum of contemporary designs and techniques. A contemporary piece may have a very traditional looking design but be made in a contemporary manner. Conversely, a traditional technique can be used with a contemporary design. And, at times there are contemporary designs made with contemporary techniques.

• History •

Appliqué is both a simple way to embellish fabric and an easy and efficient means of repairing clothing. It is a nearly international art and craft. It has long been a part of both classic and folk art traditions. In fact, the history of appliqué is almost as old as the history of textile making itself.

Appliqué is a central part of textile traditions all over the world. The most ancient example of appliquéd cloth is a ceremonial canopy dating from approximately 980 B.C. Appliqué was used to decorate wall hangings in ancient Gobi desert cultures and in ancient Egypt. In medieval Europe, appliqué was used mainly to decorate banners, horse trappings and ecclesiastical vestments. Appliqué has long been a part of the quilting traditions in the United States and Europe. There are, of course, many other examples of the use of appliqué in history—too many to list here, in fact. There are many books available about the history of appliqué specifically and textile arts in general should you wish to learn more.

• Definitions •

Appliqué: The art of applying fabric cutouts or other materials to a background in order to create a decorative pattern.

Background: Material to which motifs are appliquéd.

Basting: Stitches used to hold motifs in place on the background until secured by some means.

Decorative Stitch: A stitch used to decorate an appliqué piece as opposed to a stitch used to secure the motif in place.

Dimensional Ribbon Appliqué: Tacking pre-made ribbon-work flowers and other pre-made ribbon designs to a background.

Double-Sided Fusible Web: Often used to secure a motif to a background before stitching. A web with weak adhesive can easily be removed if desired. Different webs are made for different types of fabric.

Free-Standing Motifs: A three-dimensional design attached to a background at only one or two points.

Fused Appliqué (Bonded Appliqué): Use of fusible fabric adhesive or iron-on interfacing to bond the design to the background.

Hand-Stitched Appliqué: Hand-stitching fabric cutouts to a background.

Inlay (Mosaic): Setting a pattern into a perfectly cut background.

Iron-on Interfacing: Used to stiffen loosely woven fabrics and knits, to prevent a dark background from showing through a light foreground, or to make frayable fabrics more manageable. Creates a crisp look. Different weights are made for different types of fabric.

Machine-Stitched Appliqué: Machine-stitching fabric

cutouts to a background. Good for heavy fabrics that are difficult to hand-stitch or for items that will be used heavily or laundered frequently. Has a sharper appearance than hand-stitched appliqué.

Mixed-Media Appliqué: Use of other materials in combination with fabric to create a design. Can also refer to the use of dying and hand-painting techniques in combination with appliqué.

Motif: A piece of the appliqué design.

Padded Appliqué (3/D Appliqué): Use of some type of padding to make the appliqué more dimensional.

Reverse Appliqué (Multilayered Appliqué): Layering two or more fabrics and cutting the design out of the top layer or layers of fabric to reveal the colors beneath. It is a process of removing fabric, rather than adding fabric.

Shadow Appliqué: Placing solid-colored fabrics on a background, then covering those fabrics with sheer fabric to create a shadow effect.

Template: A reference drawing of the desired finished appliqué. It is also used to make patterns.

Turned-Edge Appliqué (Blind Appliqué): The edges of the cutout fabric turned under or hemmed before or during appliquéing them to the background. There is no stitching around the design in this method.

Step-by-step instructions for each appliqué method start on page 12. Step-by-step instructions and definitions for embroidery stitches and ribbon work start on page 17.

• Tools •

Note: The tools used are dependent upon on the means of transferring the design and the method of appliqué used for the project.

Basting thread
Cotton thread or similar synthetic thread in standard and quilting length
Craft knife
Double-sided fusible web
Dressmaker's carbon or chalk
Dressmaker's ruler
Fabric glue
Fabric marker
Florist's wire

Frame or embroidery hoop for accuracy
Iron, ironing board, pressing cloth
Iron-on interfacing
Needles: beading, embroidery, small quilting, and hand sewing; size should be appropriate for fabric
Paints and colored pencils
Pencils: hard and soft, depending on use
Photocopy machine
Pins
Ruler
Scissors: embroidery, fabric, fine-point, paper, pinking sheers, etc.
Sewing machine with embroidery function
Tape measure
Thimble
Tracing paper

• Fabrics and Threads •

All kinds of **fabrics** can be used for appliqué – plain, patterned, smooth, textured, thick and thin. The type and style of fabric used depend on the desired look of the finished product and the skill of the crafter. Cotton fabrics are the most commonly used in appliqué, and are among the easiest to use. Unwoven fabrics, like felt and leathers, are particularly easy to cut and handle and can be used by both beginner and expert alike. Other fabrics, like silks and satins, require skill and care to use but add sophistication to a piece.

The type of fabric used should be appropriate for the use of the finished piece. For instance, a piece that needs to be washed frequently should not be made from nonwashable fabrics! Furthermore, it is best to use like background fabric with like motif fabric, because they will react and behave the same way.

The type of fabric should also match the style of the piece. For example, a bright-colored felt would be just right for use in a child's wall hanging but inappropriate for a Victorian piece.

It is also important to take into account the scale of any patterns printed on fabric. Small motifs can be very versatile and will "read" even in a small piece. Larger motifs have a limited number of uses and cannot be seen if the cutout is small.

Also keep in mind how easily a fabric frays. A fabric that frays very easily may be hard to work with, and the edges will have to be secured in some way.

The above considerations for fabric choice also apply to **thread** choice. The type of thread used should be appropriate for the use and style of the finished piece.

All kinds of embroidery threads can be used for appliqué. The color and character of the thread are usually subservient to the fabric used, but not always.

Sometimes contrasting stitching adds as much to the design as the material itself.

Another consideration in choosing threads is the type of fabric used. Like threads should go with like fabrics. Natural threads should be used with natural fabrics, and synthetic threads with synthetic fabrics.

• Preparing Fabrics •

All fabrics should be clean and pressed (if possible) before using. Make certain the fabric used is preshrunk and colorfast if the finished piece will be washed. Also, check to make certain the grain line is straight by pulling out a weft thread near the edge of the fabric and cutting along the gap.

• Backing Fabrics •

A backing fabric is used as a support for fabrics that need extra firmness and strength. Most wall hangings and panels need a backing fabric, as do lightweight and stretch fabrics. The backing fabric should be prewashed and correspond in weight to the fabric it is applied to. Cut the backing fabric larger than the finished design of the appliqué to allow for seams, finishing and/or mounting. Iron-on interfacing can also be used to give body and strength to a thin fabric.

• Positioning the Design •

Most designs may be positioned simply by eye, but some need more precision. To find the center of the design, fold the paper pattern into quarters and mark two pencil lines along the folds. To check if the exact center has been located, draw a diagonal from corner to corner. If it intersects the middle of the crossed horizontal and vertical lines, you have found the exact center of the design.

The center of the fabric can be found in a similar manner. Fold the fabric in quarters and mark the lines with basting stitches. When transferring the design to the fabric, use the pencil and basting lines to check the alignment.

• Transferring the Design •

Note: It is easier to transfer the design to the back of a fabric with a pile. Make certain that you transfer a mirror image of the design.

Template: The first step in transferring the design is to make a full-scale outlined drawing of the design on tracing paper (template). Enlarge the design as needed, using a photocopier, or by hand, using dressmaker's grid paper. Number each separate part of the

design in a logical order of assembly, usually starting with the background and moving to the foreground. Use this full-scale template to mark the background, to make patterns for the motifs and as a reference during the construction of the piece.

Window or Light Table: The simplest means of marking the design on the background is tracing, using a light table or a bright window. Of course, this method only works if the background is lightweight and/or light colored.

Dressmaker's Carbon: Another means of marking the design on the background is to use dressmaker's carbon paper. Do not use office carbon paper as it will leave indelible marks. Since dressmaker's carbon comes in many colors, choose a carbon paper that is closest in color and tone to the background fabric. Be certain to follow the manufacturer's directions.

Patterns and Chalk: Another way to transfer the design is to make cardboard or paper patterns and use dressmaker's chalk, fabric markers or a soft pencil to mark the design. This method is not quite as accurate as the first two, and it is harder to mark the placement of motifs if they are not a part of the outer edge of the design.

Tracing Paper: Tracing paper can also be used to mark the outline. Pin the tracing paper to the background fabric, then pin or baste along the lines. Tear the paper away. This method is also not as accurate as tracing the design directly onto the fabric or using dressmaker's carbon.

• Making Patterns •

Note: Plan the construction of the piece carefully. Sometimes it is easier to overlap pieces than to fit them together exactly.

The tracing or the dressmaker's carbon methods can be used to transfer the design on the motif fabrics as well as the background. If neither method is feasible, patterns must be made for the motifs to ensure they are cut precisely. The pattern can be made from a variety of materials. X-ray film, stencil plastic or thick tracing paper are all good choices because they are semitransparent.

First, trace each piece of the design from the full-scale template onto tracing paper. Copy the design numbers and mark the grain lines on each piece of the design. Cut out each pattern piece. The pattern can then be transferred to a thicker material if desired.

• Cutting Out Motifs •

Cut on a flat surface so that the fabric does not pucker or draw. Be certain to add seam allowances if necessary. If using a paper pattern, pin the pattern to the fabric and cut out as with any other pattern. If using a thicker pattern, place the pattern on the fabric, pin in place, and mark the design with dressmaker's chalk, fabric markers, or a soft pencil.

• Assembling Appliqué •

When the design has been transferred to the background by tracing or with dressmaker's carbon, simply place the motifs over the marked outlines. If another means has been used, the motifs can be positioned by eye, using the full-scale template for positioning. Another way of placing the motifs is making a tracing of the design and placing it on top of the background. Then, slide the motifs between the two and pin or baste in place.

• Keeping Fabric Flat •

When doing machine appliqué, appliqué tissue is often used to hold fabric in place and prevent tiny puckers in the fabric. It is placed on the bottom layer of the fabrics to be stitched. When the stitching is complete, the paper is torn off. If no appliqué tissue is available, thick tissue paper or typing paper can be used. Even newspaper can do in a pinch.

When doing hand appliqué, good basting is essential. A motif should be basted in place with stitches running both directions to prevent the fabric from puckering. First, find the center of the fabric, then baste from the center in each direction toward the outside. Additional basting may be needed, but be certain to always start from the center to prevent any puckering of the fabric.

An embroidery hoop can be used to further hold fabric taut. If the area to be appliquéd is too large for an embroidery hoop, a frame can be used to pull fabric flat.

• Changing a Design •

The colors in the diagrams in this book are only suggestions. Remember that a design can look completely different simply by changing the colors. Also remember that the pattern and texture of the fabric used in a design will make it look different as well. Feel free to change colors, patterns and textures as desired. Many wonderful new looks can be made with the same pattern by using your imagination.

The designs in this book can also be easily mixed and matched to create new designs. Motifs from one design will often work well with motifs from another. For example, in the next column we have taken two designs and combined them to create a new design.

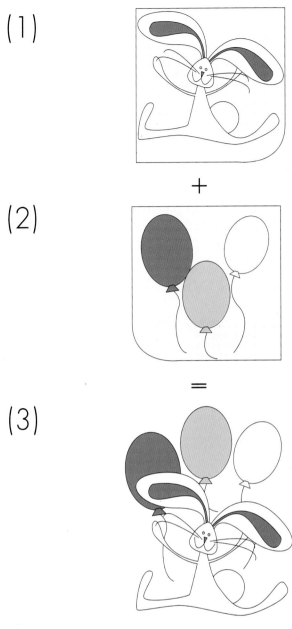

(1)

+

(2)

=

(3)

• Appliqué Methods •

The following pages contain step-by-step instructions for several different methods of appliqué. Keep in mind that appliqué techniques are often used together and one project can incorporate several methods of appliqué. The quickest method of appliqué is to combine the fused method with the machine-stitched—fusing the motifs to a background and then machine-stitching over the edges.

The more work done by hand and the more complicated the method used, the more time-consuming a project will be. A two-hour machine-stitched project would be a day's work done with hand-stitching.

Some methods of appliqué are more appropriate for certain designs than others. Choose an appliqué method that fits both the chosen design and desired finished product.

• Hand-Stitched Appliqué •

1. Place pattern right side down on wrong side of fabric. Trace and cut out shape. Label.

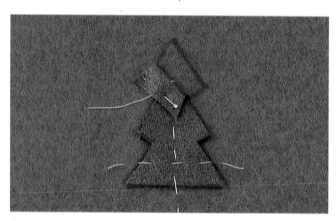

2. Mark design on background. Pin motif in place. Baste. If fabric frays easily, secure edges with overcast stitch, backstitch, or running stitch using matching thread. Remove basting stitch.

3. Stitch over edges with desired decorative stitch to conceal securing stitches. If edges do not fray, motif can be secured with stab stitching.

• Turned-Edge Appliqué • (Blind Appliqué)

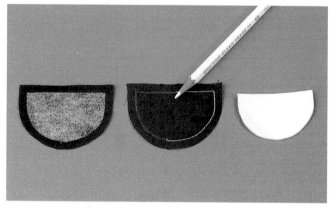

1. Trace design to fabric. Cut out motif, leaving a ⅛" to ½" seam allowance, depending on the weight of the fabric being used. (Lighter-weight fabrics need a larger seam allowance.) Machine-straight-stitch along actual motif line, or cut out iron-on interfacing to actual motif size and iron onto fabric.

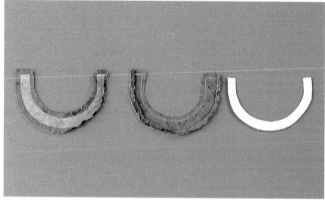

2. Fold seam allowance to wrong side, using stitching or interfacing as a guide. Snip, notch, or trim allowance as needed. Baste edges in place. Iron for a crisp, flat edge, or leave unpressed for a slight relief.

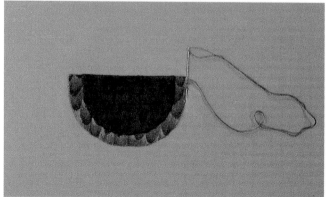

3. Mark design on fabric. Pin and baste prepared motif in place. Secure with chosen stitch. Remove basting stitches.

• Machine-Stitched Appliqué •

1. Trace motif pattern onto fabric. Cut fabric a little larger than actual design. Mark placement of motif on background. Baste onto background fabric to minimize puckering.

2. Sew over exact line with straight stitches. Trim away extra fabric. Go over stitching with a short, close zigzag or satin stitch.

3. Trim away all visible basting threads. Press to ease out any small wrinkles. Snip off raw edges and bits of thread with embroidery scissors.

• Fused Appliqué •

1. *Note: This method is most often used as a preparation for sewing rather than an independent method. Use this method without securing stitches only for infrequently used items.* Trace reverse design on nonadhesive (paper) side of double-sided fusible web (outline will be a mirror image of motif). Cut out web motif, allowing a small margin.

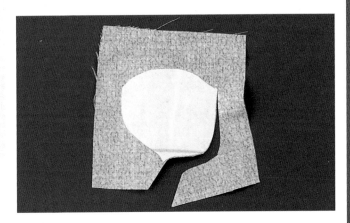

2. Iron unbacked (adhesive) side to appliqué fabric, matching grain lines and following manufacturer's instructions. Cut out motif with sharp embroidery scissors.

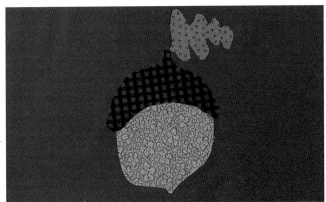

3. Mark placement of motif on background. Peel away backing paper, and iron motif to background, following manufacturer's instructions. Go over edges with machine- or hand-stitching or paint, depending on the desired finished effect and amount of use.

• Reverse Appliqué •

1. Make a template that clearly indicates colors. Cut desired pieces of fabric into identically sized pieces. Tack fabrics together. Transfer template to top layer of fabric with dressmaker's chalk. Baste around outline. Using sharp embroidery scissors, cut out layers of cloth to reveal desired color.

2. For a blind edge, leave a ¼" margin to turn under. Slip-stitch edges in place through all layers of fabric. Continue until desired effect is achieved.

3. For stitched edges, cut fabric to design outline. Machine- or hand-stitch over edges to secure. Continue until desired effect is achieved.

• Inlay •

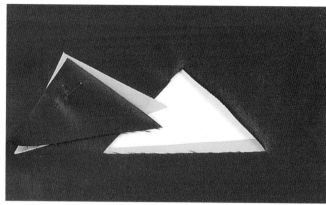

1. Mark design on right side of background fabric. Lay background fabric on top of motif fabric. Place both on a cutting board and pin in place to hold steady. Cut through both layers of fabric.

2. The traditional method of inlay is reversible. Pin and baste the fabric to a temporary backing of brown paper. Join raw edges with couched cording or buttonhole stitch, interlocking the second row with the first. The stitching should not pierce the paper. Remove paper.

3. The modern method of inlay has a backing and is not reversible. Stitch both fabrics onto backing material. Feather-stitch along joint, catching both edges and backing (a machine zigzag stitch can also be used if it is wide enough to catch both edges).

• Shadow Appliqué •

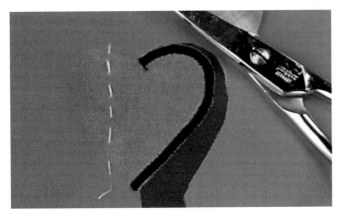

Method One: Baste a sheer fabric on top of desired shadow motif, matching grains. Draw design on sheer fabric and stitch over lines (in hand-stitching, use a pin stitch). Cut away excess sheer fabric close to stitching line. Apply to background as desired.

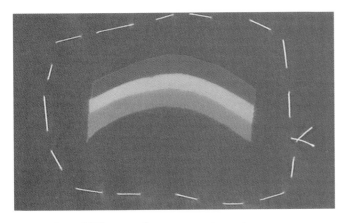

Method Two: 1. Cut motifs and secure to background as desired. Pin sheer fabric over entire design and baste around edges.

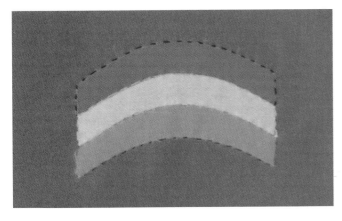

2. Work small running stitches around the edge of motifs. Either cut away fabric at lines of stitching or stitch around edges of finished piece to achieve a quilted effect.

• Padded Appliqué •

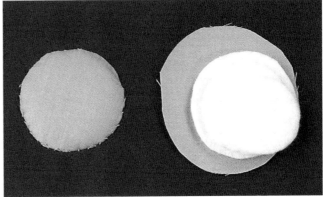

Felt: Cut out several pieces of felt the same shape as motif, each slightly smaller than the other. Starting with the smallest piece, pin and stab-stitch to center of area to be padded. Repeat with other pieces. Sew the motif* on top with turned-edge method.

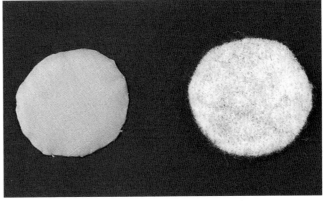

Batting: Cut required batting the same size as motif and the required thickness. Stitch batting to background with loosely tensioned straight stitches. Stitch motif* on top of batting, using turned-edge method.

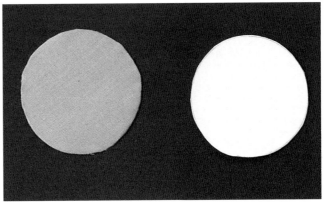

Cardboard: Cut fabric between ¼" to ½" larger than motif*. Center cardboard on wrong side of fabric. Wrap edges to back and secure with fabric glue. Slip-stitch to background around edges.

Motif must be cut slightly larger than pattern to accommodate padding.

• Mixed-Media Appliqué •

1. Buttons, beads and sequins should be sewn on in the traditional manner.

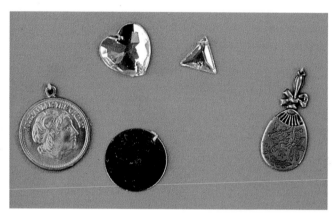

2. Other objects (like tiny mirrors or stones) can be secured with buttonhole stitching.

3. Most objects can be secured with fabric glue, tacky glue, or industrial-strength adhesive. Check to make certain the glue used will not stain fabric and will hold for desired use.

• Free-Standing Motifs •

Fusible Web: Adhere two fabrics to each other, wrong sides together. Mark design on top side and cut out shape. Stitch any details. Stiffen with fabric stiffener if desired. Motif can be shaped by inserting florist's wire between layers of fabric before bonding. Tack to background with small, invisible stitches.

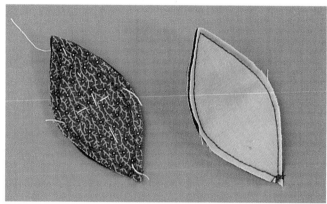

Raw Edges: 1. Mark design on top fabric. Place over bottom fabric with wrong sides together. Insert layer of batting or felt between layers if desired. Baste together. Machine-stitch along outline.

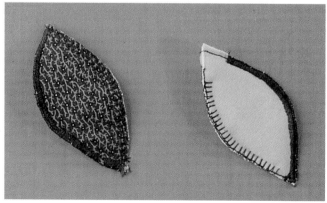

2. Cut out motif close to stitching. Work machine satin stitch or close zigzag stitch along edge, or cover with hand-stitched buttonhole stitch.

• Dimensional Ribbon Appliqué •

1. *Note: Ribbon work instructions are on page 19. Specific projects in Chapter 3 may also give instructions in ribbon appliqué. Make all desired ribbon pieces, such as flower, leaf or bow. Mark placement on background, taking care to note which layer should be attached first if necessary.*

2. Tack ribbon piece on background, using small invisible stitches, like a slip stitch or hem stitch.

If you do not wish to make your own dimensional ribbon items, several companies offer pre-made ribbon flowers and bows for purchase. These can be found at most sewing, needlework, and crafts stores.

Silk, velvet, and lace flowers can also be appliquéd, using the dimensional ribbon technique. You can also mix and match ribbon, silk, velvet, and lace flowers for an interesting design.

The ribbon flowers and motifs used in this book are described beginning on page 19. If you cannot find the kind of ribbon flowers you want to make in our instructions, there are several good ribbon craft books that illustrate how to make many kinds of dimensional ribbon crafts. Feel free to explore and experiment!

• Embroidery Stitches •

The following are instructions for many common embroidery stitches, but there are many, many more. Several excellent stitch dictionaries are available that catalog hundreds of different stitches if a different stitch is desired.

• Backstitch
Come up at A; go down at B, to the right of A. Come up at C, to the left of A. Repeat B-C, inserting the needle in the same hole.

• Blanket Stitch
A blanket stitch is worked like a buttonhole stitch, except a space is left between each upright.

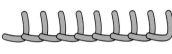

•Buttonhole Stitch
(1) Bring needle up at A, down at B. Bring needle up again at C, keeping thread under needle.
(2) For second stitch, go down at D and back up at E.
(3) Completed Buttonhole Stitch.

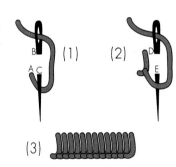

• Crossed Buttonhole Stitch
(1) Come up at A, go down at B and up at A. Go down at C and up at D, with tip of needle over thread, and pull to complete stitch.
(2) Go down at E and up at D. Go down at F and up at G, with tip of needle over thread, and pull to complete stitch. Continue to end of row.
(3) Completed Crossed Buttonhole Stitch.

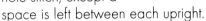

• Chain Stitch
(1) Bring needle up at A. Put needle down through fabric at B and back up at C, keeping thread under needle to form a loop. Pull thread

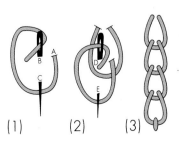

through, making a loop.

(2) To form the next chain loop which holds the previous one in place, go down at D and back up at E. Continue to form each loop in the same manner.

(3) Completed Chain Stitch. Finish with a short straight stitch over the bottom of the last loop to secure.

• Couching Stitch

(1) Complete a straight-stitch base by coming up at A and going down at B (the desired length of the straight stitch).

(2) Make a short, tight straight stitch across the base to "couch" the straight stitch. Come up at C on one side of the thread. Go down at D on the opposite side of the thread. The straight-stitch base is tacked at varying intervals.

(3) Completed Couching Stitch.

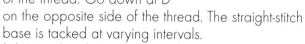

• Feather Stitch

(1) Come up at A. Go down at B and back up at C, keeping the thread under the needle to hold it in a "V" shape. Pull flat.

(2) For second stitch, go down at D and back up at E.

(3) Completed Feather Stitch.

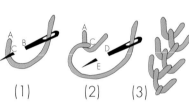

(1)   (2)   (3)

• Running Stitch

A line of straight stitches with an unstitched area between each stitch. Come up at A and go down at B.

A BA BA BA B

• Satin Stitch

(1) Come up at A and go down at B, forming a straight stitch. Then come up at C and go down again at B, forming another smooth straight stitch that is slightly overlapping the first.

(2) Repeat to fill design area.

(1)   (2)

• Slip Stitch

A small straight stitch worked from the background fabric into the edge of the motif, at tight angles to the motif's edge.

• Stab Stitch

A Stab Stitch forms a dotted line, with tiny stitches evenly spaced in a line. It differs from running stitch in that the needle pierces the fabric vertically instead of diagonally.

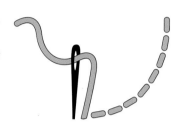

• Stem Stitch

Working from left to right, make slightly slanting stitches along the line of the stem. Come up at A and insert needle through fabric at B. Bring needle up at C (halfway between A and B). Make all stitches the same length. Insert needle through fabric at D (half the length of the stitch beyond B). Bring needle up at the middle of previous stitch and continue in the same manner.

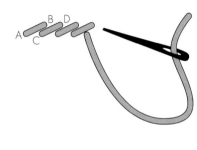

• Whipped Running Stitch

(1) Complete the Running Stitches first.

(2) To whip the running stitch, go under the first running stitch from A to B. (Be careful not to pierce the fabric or catch the running stitch.) Come up on the other side of the stitch. Wrap the thread over the stitch and go under the next running stitch at C. Continue in the same manner. The effect can be varied by how loosely or tightly the thread is pulled when whipping.

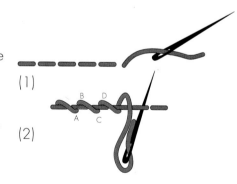

Note: When working whipping, it is good to use a blunt-end needle or put needle through running stitches eye first to avoid catching the thread.

• Ribbon Work •

Individual instructions will include ribbon required for the project and other information as needed.

• Cascading Stitch

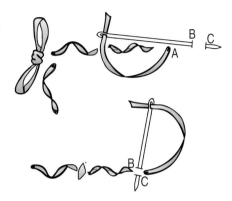

The Cascading Stitch can be done starting with a bow or just using ribbon to "cascade" streamers through design. If starting with a bow, tie bow, leaving streamers long enough to work "cascade" through design. Thread streamer on needle, stitch down through fabric where bow placement is desired and come back up at start of "cascade" effect. This will hold the bow in place.

(1) Come up at A and go down at B. Come back up at C, allowing ribbon to twist and lay loosely on the fabric.

(2) Go down again at B and come up at C, making a small backstitch. This keeps the cascading in place.

• Daffodil

(1) Petals: Cut six 2¾" lengths from 1½"-wide sheer yellow to orange ombré wired ribbon. To make one petal, cut the short sides at an angle so that top edge is 2¾" and bottom edge is 1" (bottom edge is bright orange).

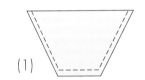

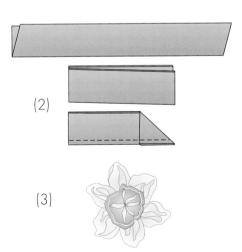

Gather-stitch side and bottom. Pull gathers and secure. Make five more petals. Chain petals together, pull gathering thread lightly and secure. Join last petal to first petal.

(2) Center: Cut a 5" length from the same ribbon. Fold in half, then fold in half again. Fold raw edge at a 45° angle and gather-stitch folded edge. Pull gathering thread tightly and secure. Sew the gathered edge to the center of the petals.

(3) Completed Daffodil.

• Folded Leaf

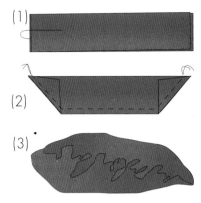

(1) Fold a 7" length of 1"-wide ombré ribbon in half.

(2) Fold corner to form 45° angles. Gather along darker edge of ombré.

(3) Pull slightly and tie off. Trim bulk from corners and open leaf.

• Free-Form Flower Stitch

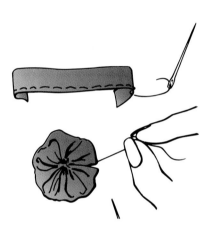

(1) Use a 2" piece of ribbon. Fold each end under about ⅛". Baste along one long edge of the ribbon with one strand of sewing thread or floss.

(2) Gather ribbon tightly to create a flower. Knot to secure ruffled effect. Stitch ribbon in place along the gathered edge.

• French Knot

(1) Bring needle up through fabric at A; smoothly wrap ribbon once around needle.

(2) Hold ribbon securely off to one side, and push needle down through fabric at B.

(3) Completed French Knots.

• Fuchsia

(1) Cut a 6½" length of 1½"-wide wired ribbon. Fold ribbon in half with short ends together. Crease ribbon on fold to mark center. Fold one end of ribbon to center, overlapping ¼". Fold remaining end down ¼". Fold to meet center and pin.

(2) Draw a diamond with disappearing pen. Points are $\frac{1}{16}$" from edge. Knot end of 2mm ribbon. Stitch through center of ribbon for stem. Fold stamen in half and hot-glue to inside of fuchsia.

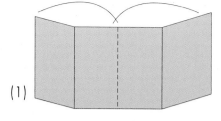

(1)

(2)

(3)

Gather-stitch diamond. Pull tight and tie off.
(3) Completed Fuchsia.

• Ivy Leaf
(1) Cut 1"-wide ribbon into a 7" or a 5" length. Gather-stitch each as shown.

(1)   (2)

(2) Pull thread tightly. Appliqué in place, shaping petal like an ivy leaf.

• Layered Pointed-Petal Flower
(1) Cut 1½"-wide wired ribbon into fifteen 6" lengths.
(2) Make pointed petals by folding one edge at a 45° angle and the other edge over first angel at a 45° angle. Gather-stitch below the salvage.

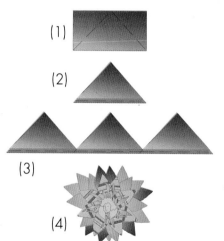

(1)

(2)

(3)

(4)

(3) Chain together, pull gathers as tightly as possible and secure. Join to first petal. Secure thread and tie off.
(4) To make second layer, cut 1½" striped wired ribbon into twelve 6" pieces. Make 12 petals. Gather-stitch, catching salvage. Chain together, pull gathers as tightly as possible and secure. Join to first petal, secure thread and tie off.

Sew second petal layer to first. Using industrial-strength adhesive, glue a charm in the flower center.

• Lazy Daisy
(1) Bring the needle up at A. Keep the ribbon flat, un-

twisted and full. Put the needle down through fabric at B and up through at C, keeping the ribbon under the needle to form a loop. Pull the ribbon through, leaving the loop loose and full. To hold the loop in place, go down on other side of ribbon near C, forming a straight stitch over loop.
(2) Completed Lazy Daisy.

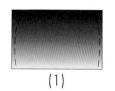

(1)

(2)

• Japanese Ribbon Stitch
(1) Come up through fabric at the starting point of stitch. Lay the ribbon flat on the fabric. At the end of the stitch, pierce the ribbon with the needle. Slowly pull the length of the ribbon through to the back, allowing the ends of the ribbon to curl. If the ribbon is pulled too tight, the effect of the stitch can be lost. Vary the petals and leaves by adjusting the length, the tension of the ribbon before piercing, the position of piercing, and how loosely or tightly the ribbon is pulled down through itself.
(2) Completed Japanese Ribbon Stitch.

• Mum
(1) Cut a 22½" and a 17 ½" length of ribbon. Measure and mark 22½" length of ribbon following diagram.
(2) Fold downward at each mark. Gather-stitch as shown. Pull thread tightly and secure. Repeat with 17½" length of ribbon with only five 2½"-long intervals. Stitch larger petals in place with embroidery floss, then stitch smaller petals

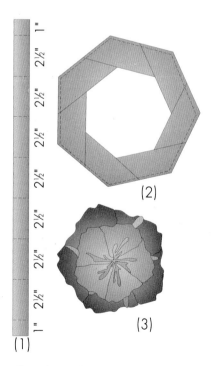

(2)

(3)

(1)

on top. Make small stitches throughout flower for texture.
(3) Completed Mum.

• Rosette
(1) Cut a 12" piece of 9mm ribbon. Fold ribbon at a 45° angle with ½" tail. Fold again.

(2) Fold edge of ribbon diagonally back and wrap around center. Secure each wrap with thread. Continue to wrap and roll for half of the ribbon.

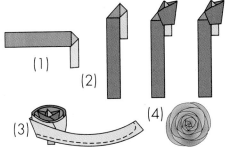

(1)

(2)

(3)

(4)

(3) Gather bottom edge of remaining ribbon tapering thread at end. Pull up gathers and wrap around rose. Secure.

(4) Completed Rosette.

• Straight Stitch

This stitch may be taut or loose, depending on desired effect.

(1) Come up at A. Go down at B, keeping the ribbon flat.

(2) Completed Straight Stitch.

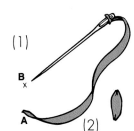

(1)

B
x

A

(2)

• Strawberry

(1) Cut a 4" length of 1½"-wide red ribbon and a 3" length of ¼"-wide single-faced light olive satin. Fold red ribbon in half. Make a diagonal cut in the ribbon so that the bottom measures ¾" and the top 2". Stitch the diagonal together and turn to right side.

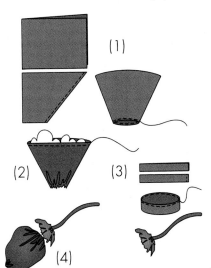

(1)

(2)

(3)

(4)

Make a running stitch along the bottom. Pull tight and secure gathers.

(2) Lightly stuff strawberry with a small amount of batting. Gather-stitch top edge of strawberry and secure gathers.

(3) Fold ¼"-wide olive satin in half. Stitch seam and turn. Gather-stitch top edge. Tie a knot in one end of 2mm rattail, and place throughout center of olive gathered edge so that the knot is on the inside for stem. Stitch gathers and rattail securely in place.

(4) Tack olive satin to strawberry. Pin completed strawberry to background, being careful to make tacks as invisible as possible. Lightly shape and mold strawberry with french knots, using three strands of olive brown embroidery floss.

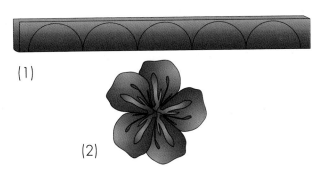

(1)

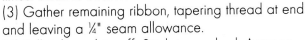

(2)

• Violet

(1) Cut a 7½" length of 1"-wide shaded violet silk ribbon. Fold in half lengthwise and press. Trace a half circle five times on ribbon, leaving ¼" at beginning and end. Gather-stitch along each half circle. Pull as tight as possible and secure thread. Join to first petal and secure thread. Adjust petals as needed.

(2) Completed Violet.

• Wisteria

Make twelve 3" petals like a rosette.

(1) Fold 1½"-wide fabric at a 45° angle.

(2) Fold again. Roll fabric three times. Stitch to secure.

(3) Gather remaining ribbon, tapering thread at end and leaving a ¼" seam allowance.

(4) Pull tight and tie off. Stitch to rosebud. Arrange petals, following diagram on page 122.

(1)

(2)

(3)

(4)

• Painting Techniques and Tips •

Painting on fabric requires a textile medium. A textile medium is mixed with acrylic paint to make it glide better over fabric and make it permeate the fibers. It prevents paint from bleeding and makes the painting, when dry, permanent.

Fabric should be washed before painting and then ironed smooth. The fabric should then be stretched taut to prevent any bubbling or puckering. See page 11 for ideas on keeping fabric flat.

To use a textile medium, first pour a small amount of desired paint onto palette. Place a few drops of medium onto paint. Mix well. The paint will become more transparent as more textile medium is added. Paint can also be diluted with water. Paint. After the paint is dry, most fabrics painted with textile medium can be heat-set in a dryer or with a warm iron on the reverse side of fabric. *Make certain to read and follow manufacturer's instructions when using a textile medium.*

2

Traditional appliqué includes most appliqué work done on a fabric background. This chapter has pieces suitable for framing, charming pillows, cute banners, and perfect Christmas decorations.

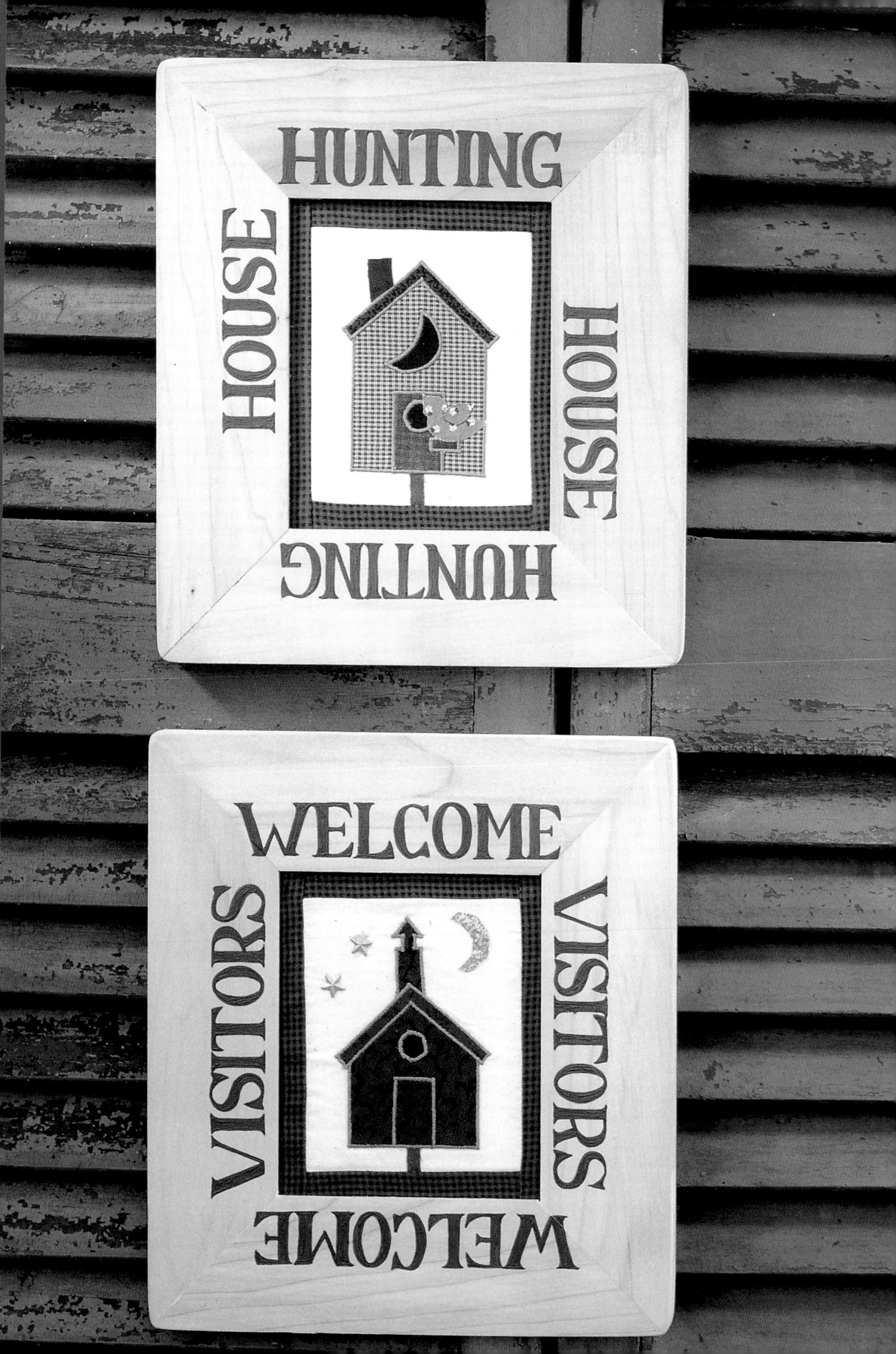

Model Information

Method: Machine-Stitched
Enlargement: 125%
Fabrics: Cottons and Muslin
Note: Star charms were used on bottom right house.

FOR SALE
APARTMENT FOR WRENT
VISITORS WELCOME
HOUSE HUNTING

Framed Birdhouses Patterns

Every seed after its own kind

BE ONE OF A KIND

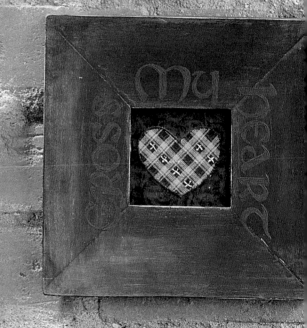

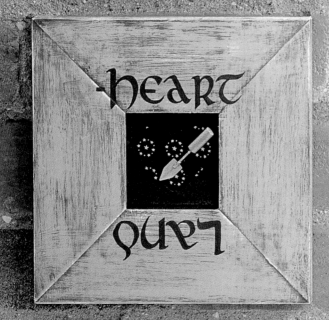

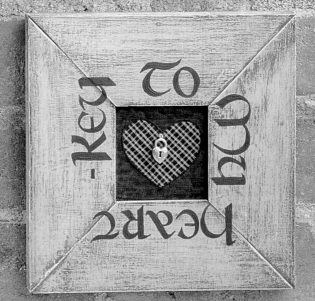

Model Information

Method: Machine-Stitched
Enlargement: Actual Size
Fabrics: Cotton Calicos
Note: Charms were added to appliqué to go along with heart sayings.

Framed Heart and Broken Heart Patterns

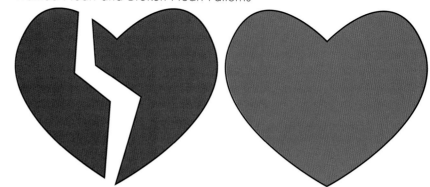

Additional Designs

Additional Designs

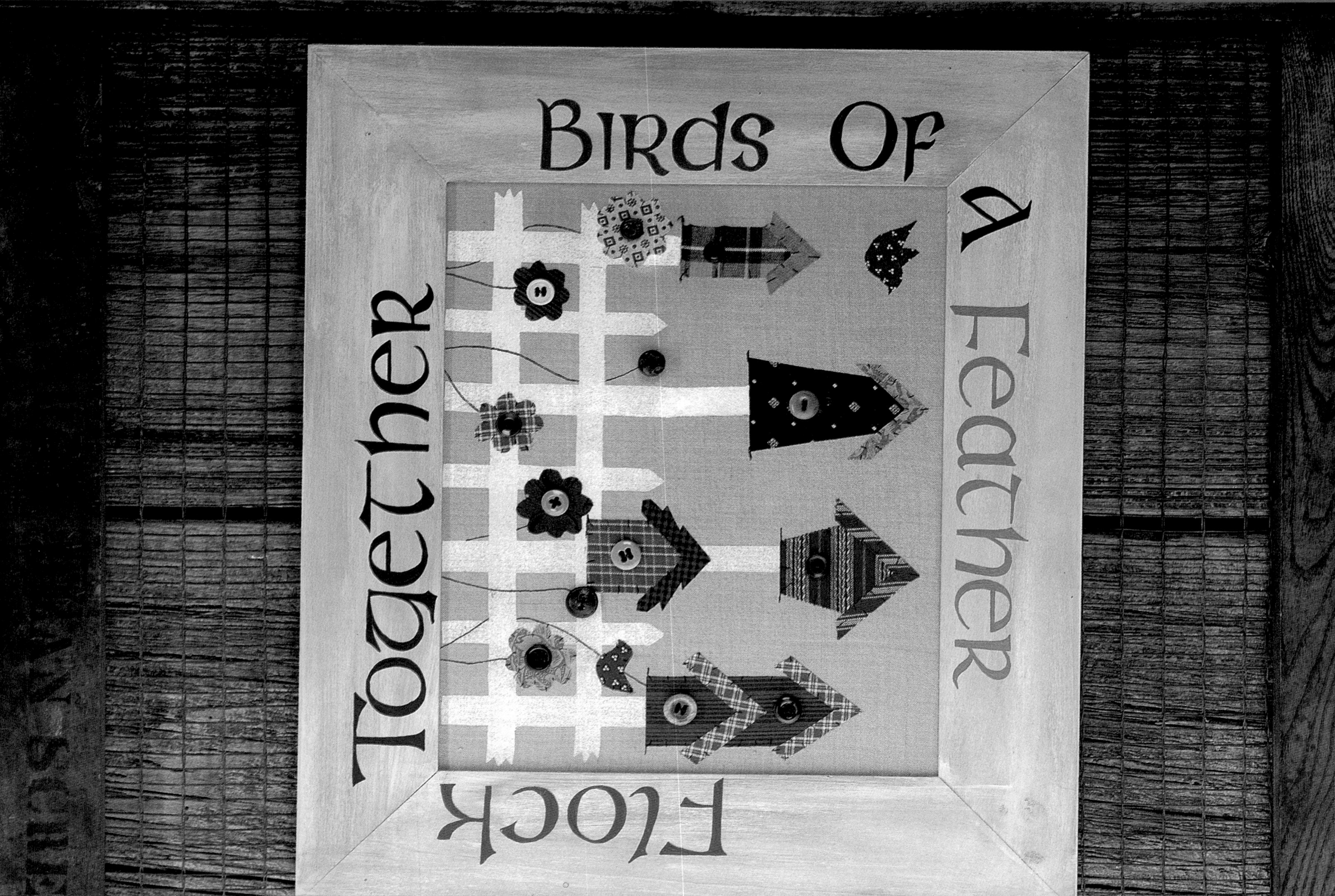
Birds Of
A Feather
Flock
Together

Framed
Picket
Fence and
Birdhouses
Pattern

Model Information

Method: Machine-Stitched
Enlargement: 190%
Fabrics: Printed Cottons
*Notes: Picket fence was stenciled
    on fabric with diluted white
    acrylic paint. Buttons were used
    for flower centers.*

Additional Design

Additional Designs

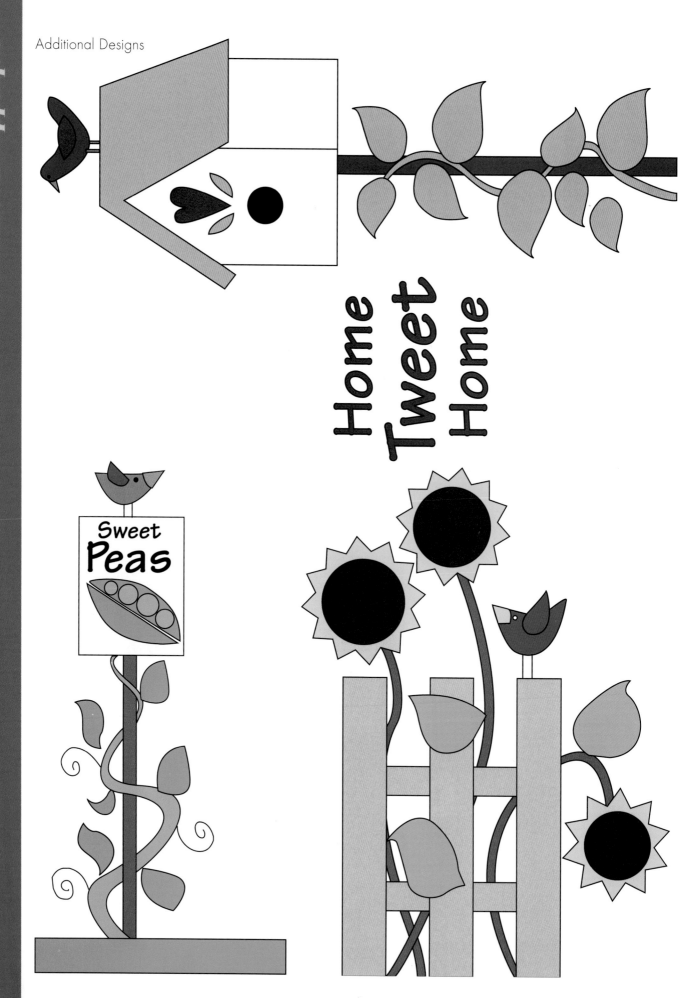

Home Tweet Home

Sweet **Peas**

Additional Designs

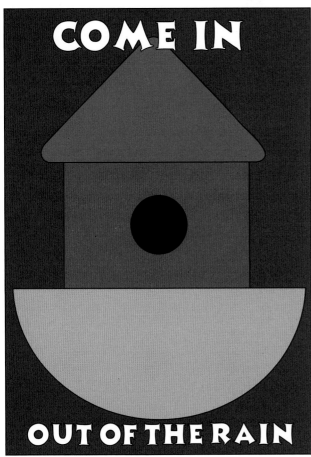

HANDS TO
WORK
HEARTS TO
GOD

LA NUIT

Sweet
Pea

From My Garden Pattern

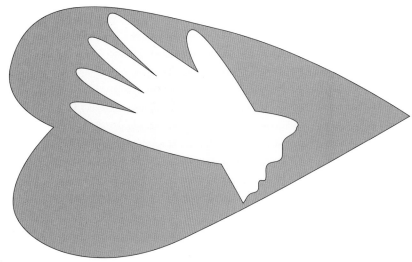

Sweet Pea Pattern

Sweet Pea

La Nuit Alphabet

ABCDEFGHIJ
KLMNOPQRS
TUVWXYZ

Model Information

From My Garden
Method: Fused, Hand-Stitched
    details
Enlargement: 215%
Fabrics: Polished Cotton and
    Muslin
*Note: Several lengths of coor-
    dinating 4mm silk ribbons
    were stitched to cuff and
    tied around ribbon flowers.*

Sweet Pea
Method: Machine-Stitched
Enlargement: 200%
Fabrics: Printed Cottons

La Nuit
Method: Machine-Stitched
Enlargement: 125%
Fabrics: Poly-Cotton Blends

Hands to Work
Method: Machine-Stitched
Enlargement: 160%
Fabrics: Printed Poly-Cotton
    Blends
*Notes: Buttons were used to
    outline right heart. Lace
    was used for the cuff of the
    glove.*

Hands to Work Pattern

HANDS TO
WORK
HEARTS TO
GOD

Additional Designs

Just
between the
moon & you-
angels get
a better view.

Lemonade!

Have your cake
and
Eat it too!

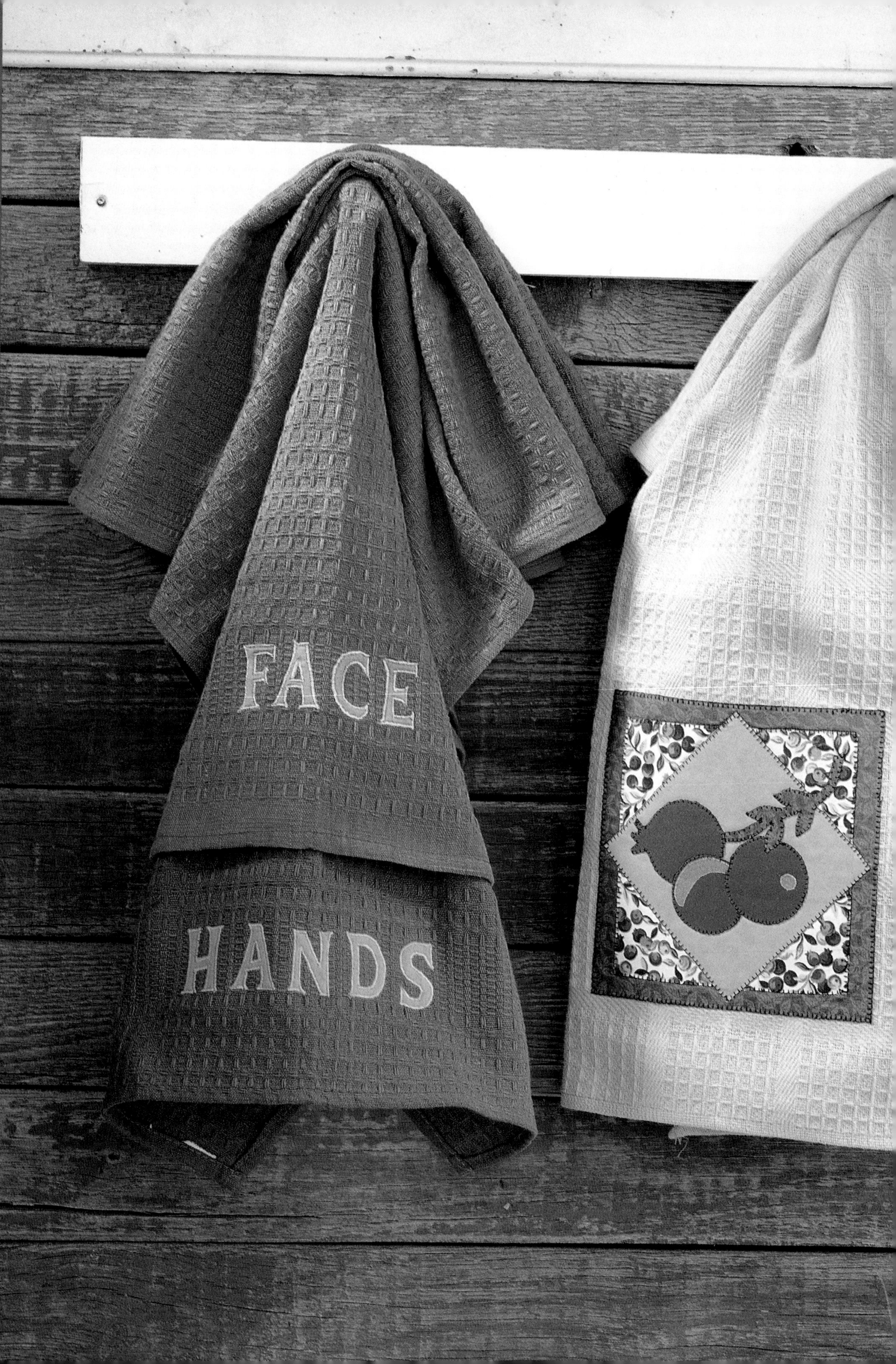
FACE
HANDS

Model Information

Blueberry and Strawberry
Method: Fused and Machine-Stitched
Enlargement: 180%
Fabrics: Cotton and Poly-Cotton Blends

Hands and Face
Method: Fused and Machine-Stitched
Enlargement: 210%
Fabrics: Cotton

Sunflowers
Method: Fused and Machine-Stitched
Enlargement: 190%
Fabrics: Cotton Calicos

Additional Design

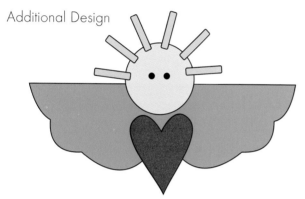

It all starts
with a
little miracle!

Hands and Face Pattern

A B C D E F G H I J K
L M N O P Q R S T U
V W X Y Z

Blueberry and Strawberry Pattern

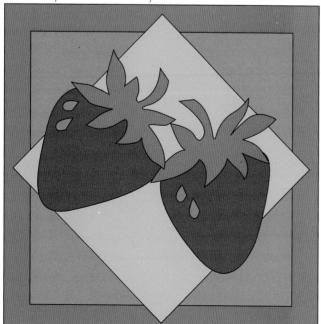

Model Information

Rex Rabbit Sweatshirt
Method: Fused
Enlargement: 215%
Fabrics: Cotton Blends

Rex Rabbit Tote Bag
Method: Fused and
    Machine-Stitched
Enlargement: 230%
Fabrics: Cotton Blends

Rex Rabbit Sweatshirt Pattern

Rex Rabbit Tote Bag Pattern

Share my garden

Share my heart.

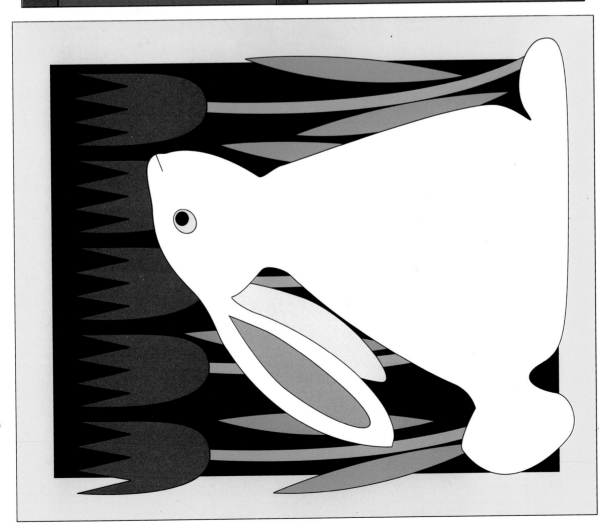

Model Information

Forever Friends
Method: Padded, Fused, and Machine-Stitched
Enlargement: 510%
Fabrics: Screen-printed Cottons and Cotton Calicos

Joy to the World
Method: Fused and Machine-Stitched
Enlargement: 230%
Fabrics: Cotton Calicos

Apple of My Pie
Method: Fused and Machine-Stitched
Enlargement: 190%
Fabrics: Printed Cottons
Note: Lazy Daisy stitches and a button were stitched on pie crust.

Happy Halloween
Method: Fused and Hand-Stitched
Enlargement: 225%
Fabrics: Poly-Cotton Blends and Screen-Printed Background

Forever Friends Pattern

Joy to the World Pattern

Apple of My
Pie Pattern

Happy
Halloween
Pattern

Additional Design

Queen
for a day

Long Live
the
Queen!

**Do you love me
Do you not
You told me once
But I forgot.**

NOT
A PEEP OUT
OF ANY
OF
YOU!

Model Information

Juggling Cat
Method: Fused
Enlargement: 200%
Fabrics: Poly-Cotton Blends.
Note: Ceramic buttons were used as juggling balls

Jester
Method: Fused with Painted Stitch Lines
Enlargement: 170%
Fabrics: Screen-Printed Cottons
Note: Jester's face was made with acrylic paints.

Birdhouse
Method: Fused and Machine-Stitched
Enlargement: 250%
Fabrics: Cotton Calicos and Lace

Patriot Bears
Method: Fused with Fabric Pen Stitch Lines
Enlargement: 175%
Fabrics: Cottons (Screen-Print, Polished, Broadcloth, etc.)

Jester Pattern

Juggling Cat Pattern

Birdhouse Pattern

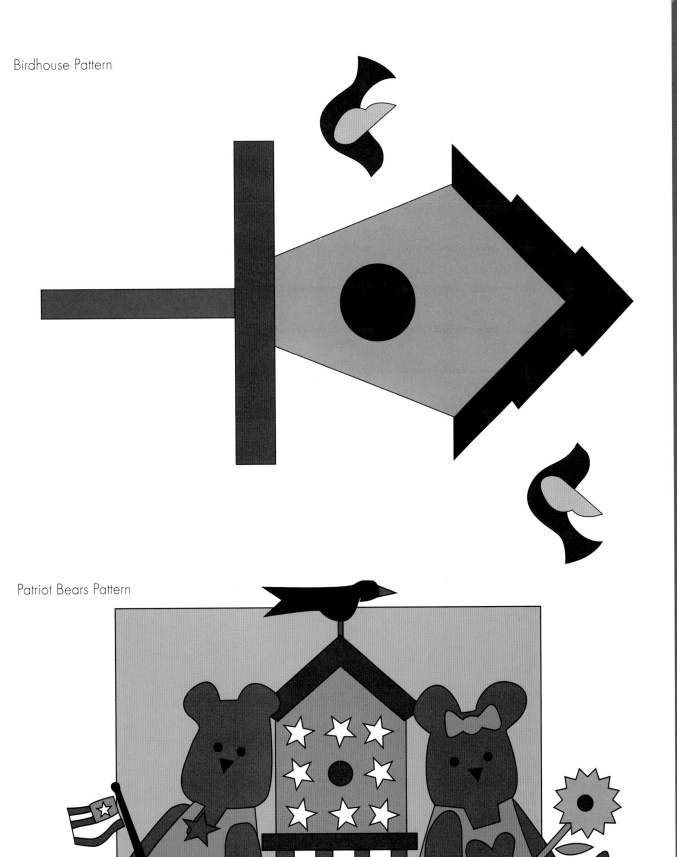

Patriot Bears Pattern

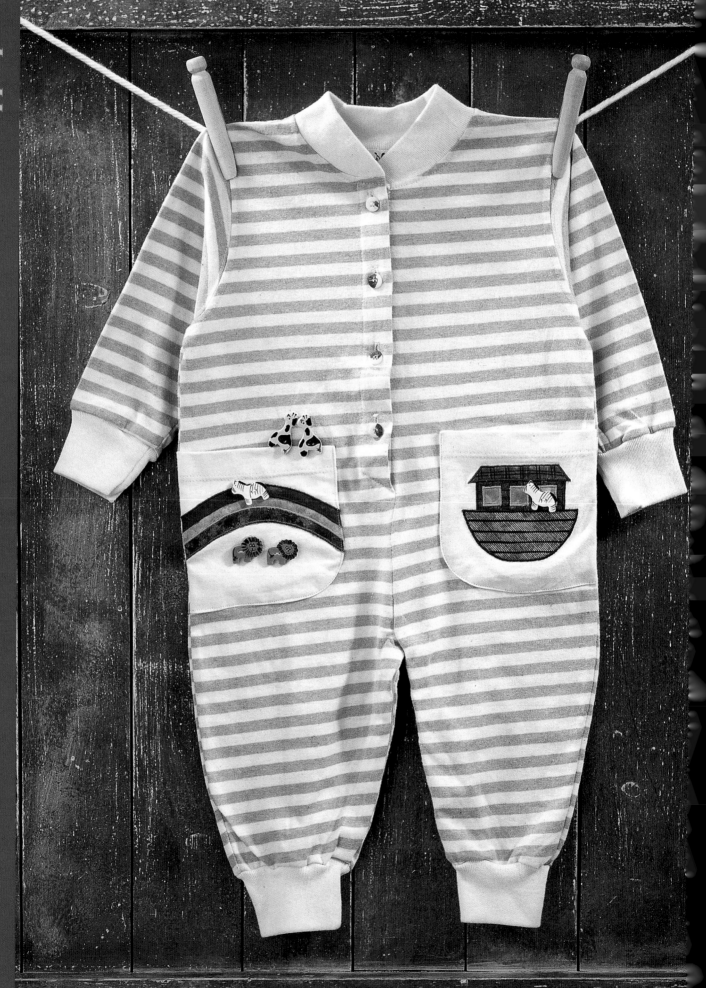

Model Information

Method: Fused and Machine-
  Stitched
Enlargement: 220%
Fabrics: Cotton Calicos
*Note: Ceramic animal buttons
were stitched to pockets.*

Additional Designs

Noah's Ark Pajamas Pattern

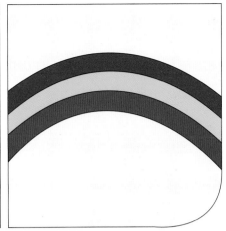

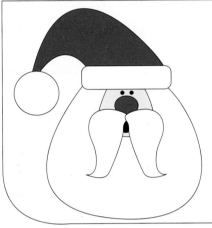

• Traditional Appliqué

Model Information

Method: Hand- and Machine-Stitched
Enlargement: 200%
Fabrics: Cotton Calicos

all hearts go home
·
for Christmas

All Hearts Go Home Pattern

Model Information

Additional Design

Merry Christmas Wreath Banner

Method: Fused and Machine-Stitched
Enlargement: 240%
Fabrics: Printed Cottons
Notes: Washable taffeta ribbons were used on the banner. Metallic red machine embroidery thread was used on berries.

Snow Angels Banner

Method: Fused and Machine-Stitched
Enlargement: 340%
Fabrics: Felts and Screen-Printed Cottons.
Notes: Sequins were used for snowflake centers and seed beads for snow angels' eyes and mouths.

Merry Christmas Wreath Banner Pattern

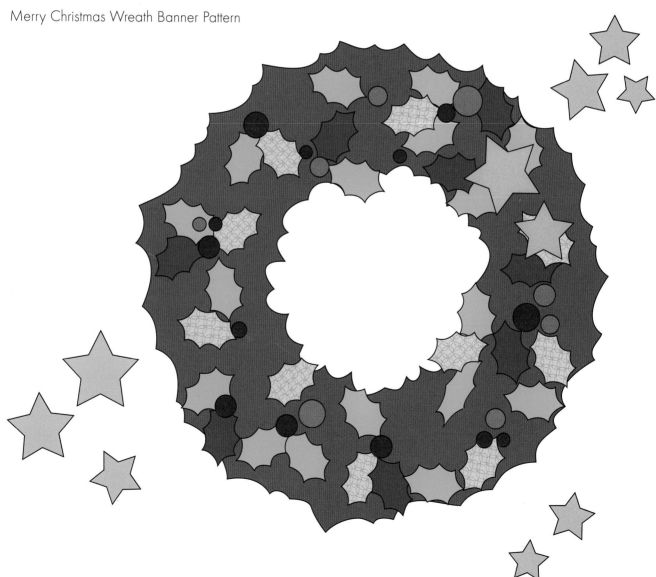

Snow Angels Banner Pattern

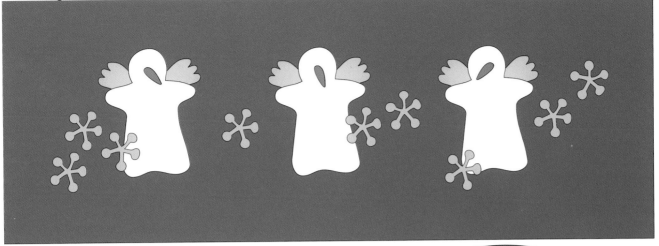

Additional Designs

LIGHTS FADE
STARS APPEAR
EVENING ANGELS
GATHER HERE.

Alleluia

Model Information

Method: Fused, and Hand- and Machine-Stitched
Enlargement: 200%
Fabrics: Cotton Calicos on a Cotton Rug

Additional
Designs

Yuletide Table Runner
Pattern

HO
HO
HO

Model Information

Christmas Knit Stockings
Method: Hand-Stitched
Enlargement: 265%
Fabrics: Knit Stocking and Felt Motifs

Felt Christmas Tree Skirt
Method: Fused and Hand-Stitched
Enlargement: 510%
Fabrics: Felt

Felt Christmas Stocking
Method: Fused and Hand-Stitched
Enlargement: 270%
Fabrics: Felt

Felt Christmas Tree Skirt
Pattern

Christmas Knit Stockings Pattern

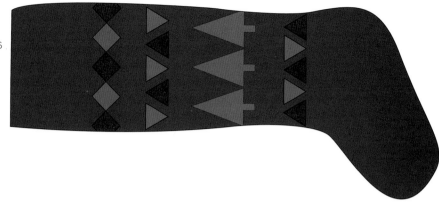

Felt Christmas Stockings Patterns

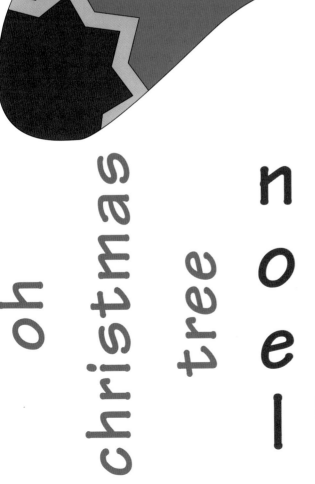

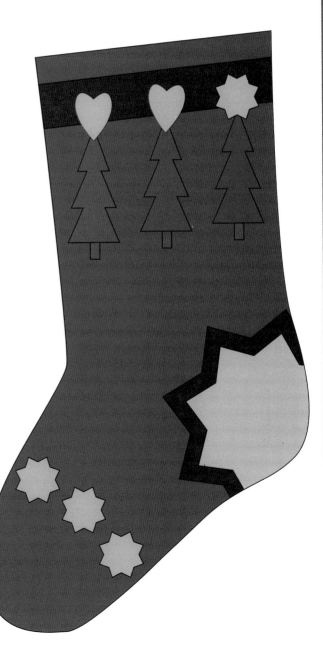

abcdef
ghijklm
nopqrs
tuvwxyz

oh christmas tree

noel

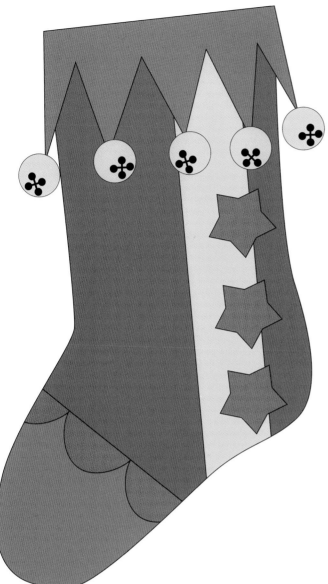

a b c d e
f g h i j k
l m n o p
q r s t u
v w x y z

**happy
holidays**

**have a
cool yule**

3

Contemporary appliqué includes mixed-media, dimensional ribbon, and painted appliqué. This kind of appliqué also includes appliquéing to a nonfabric background such as paper or wood.

Model Information

Cowboy Bags
Method: Fused Appliqué
Enlargement: 145%
Fabrics: Denim, Bandanna,
    and Gold Metallic

Holiday Ornaments Bag
Method: Fused Appliqué
Enlargement: 190%
Fabrics: Vinyl Coated Metallic
    or Wrapping Paper, and
    Gold Metallic Lace
*Note: Cording was used for
    ornament "hangers."*

Cowboy Bags Patterns

KICK UP YOUR HEELS

These boots are made for walking-

Share my garden

Share my heart...

Model Information

Teacher Box Pattern

Teacher Box
Method: Fused Appliqué
Enlargement: 160%
Fabrics: Cotton Calicos

Christmas Box
Method: Fused Appliqué
Enlargement: 145%
Fabrics: Cotton Calicos and
Cotton twill

*Notes: The sides of both boxes
were appliquéd with coordi-
nating fabric. Additional stars
were randomly appliquéd to
sides. Pencils were glued to
teacher box with industrial-
strength adhesive.*

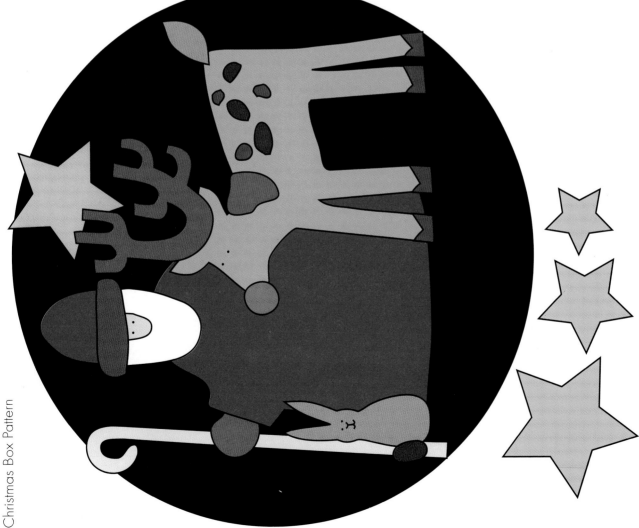

Christmas Box Pattern

• Contemporary Appliqué

Here
Kitty
Kitty

HEARTS
over easy

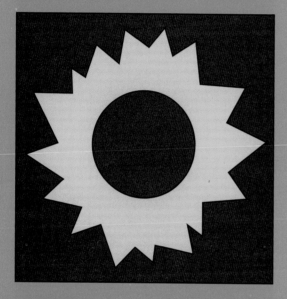

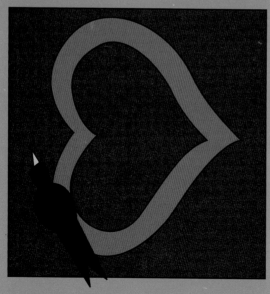

Model Information

Hearts & Sunflowers Panel
Method: Fused Appliqué
Enlargement: 290%
Fabrics: Cotton Calicos

Sunflower Clock
Method: Fused Appliqué
Enlargement: 150%
Fabrics: Cotton Calicos

• Clocks •

Materials

¾"-thick wooden circle (model was 9" in diameter)
Clock movement and hands
Acrylic paints
Paintbrushes and sponges
Drill

Instructions

1. Paint clock face as desired with acrylic paints (model was sponge-painted). Let dry. Apply double-sided fusible web to appliqué motifs, following general instructions and manufacturer's instructions. Iron motifs onto clock face, being careful not to touch painted surface with hot iron.

2. Drill a hole for clock movement in center of clock face, according to size of clock movement and manufacturer's instructions. Assemble clock movement and attach clock hands, according to manufacturer's instructions.

Additional Design

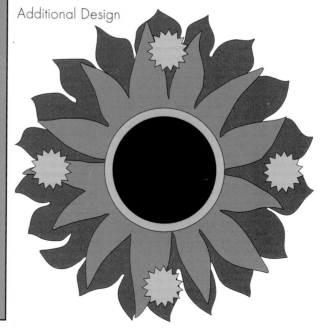

Sunflower Clock Pattern

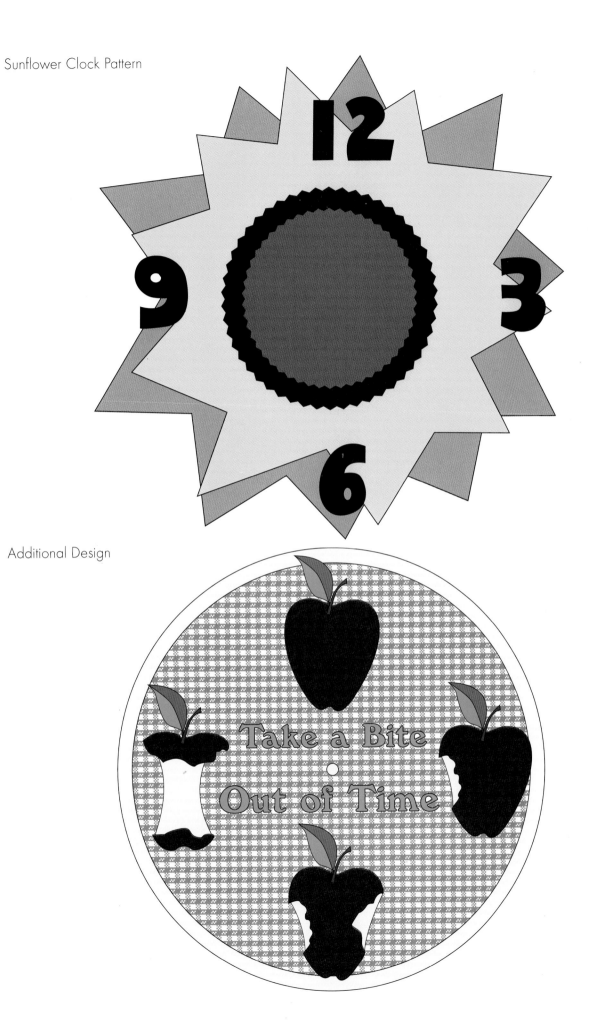

Additional Design

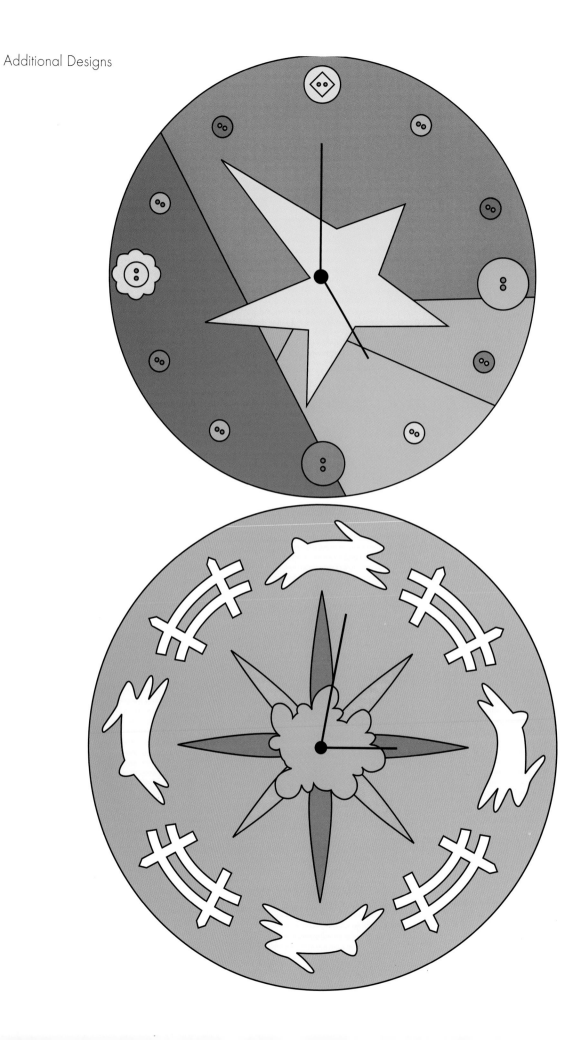

Model Information

Folk Cow Door Topper
Method: Fused Appliqué
Enlargement: 235%
Fabrics: Cotton, Broadcloth, and Muslin

Folk Cow Door
Topper Pattern

Chicken and Corn
Method: Fused Appliqué
Enlargement: 185%
Fabrics: Cotton Calicos
Note: Additional corn motifs were appliquéd to frame.

Chicken and Corn Pattern

WELCOME TO OUR PAD

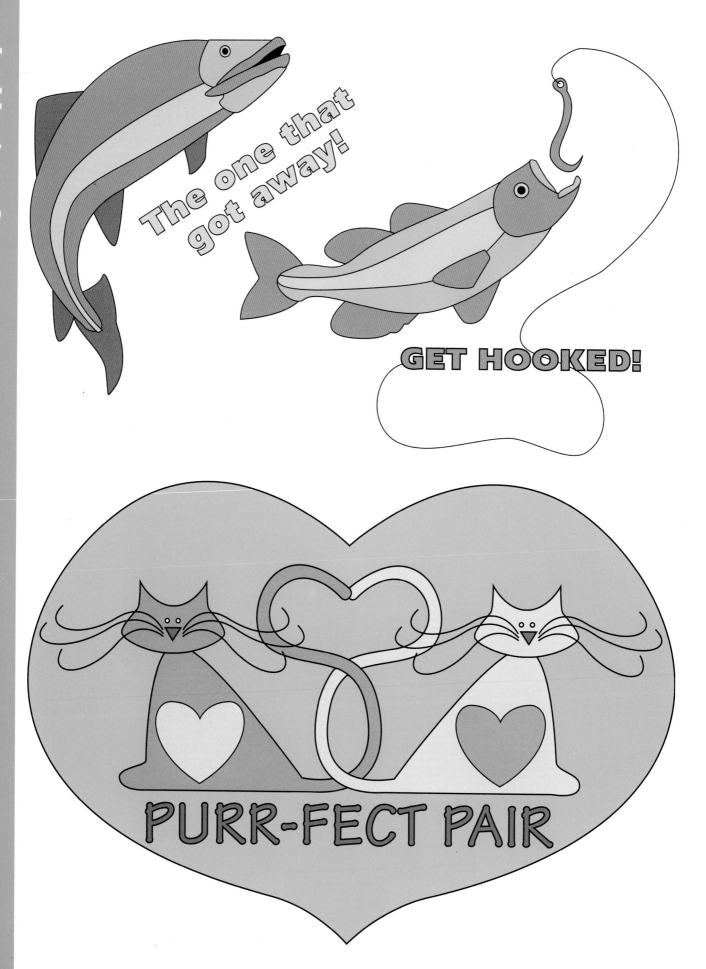

Model Information

Pieced-Heart Vest
Method: Machine-Stitched Appliqué
Enlargement: 155%
Fabrics: Cotton Calicos

Painted Vest
Method: Mixed Media
Enlargement: Actual Size
Fabrics: Cottons with Acrylic Paints mixed with Textile
Medium (see page 21)

Pieced-Heart Vest Pattern

Painted Vest Patterns (face and bars)

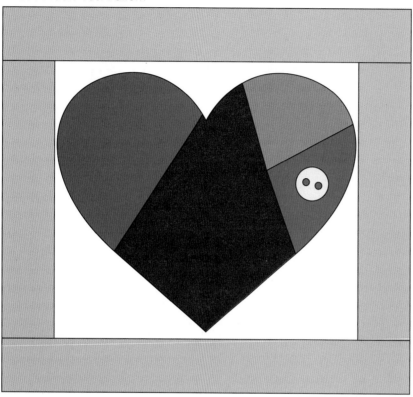

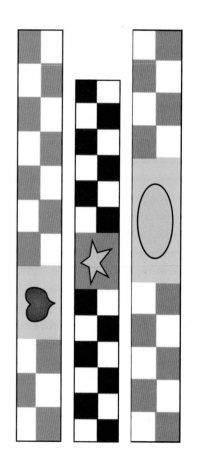

Painted Vest Patterns (Heart)

Additional Designs

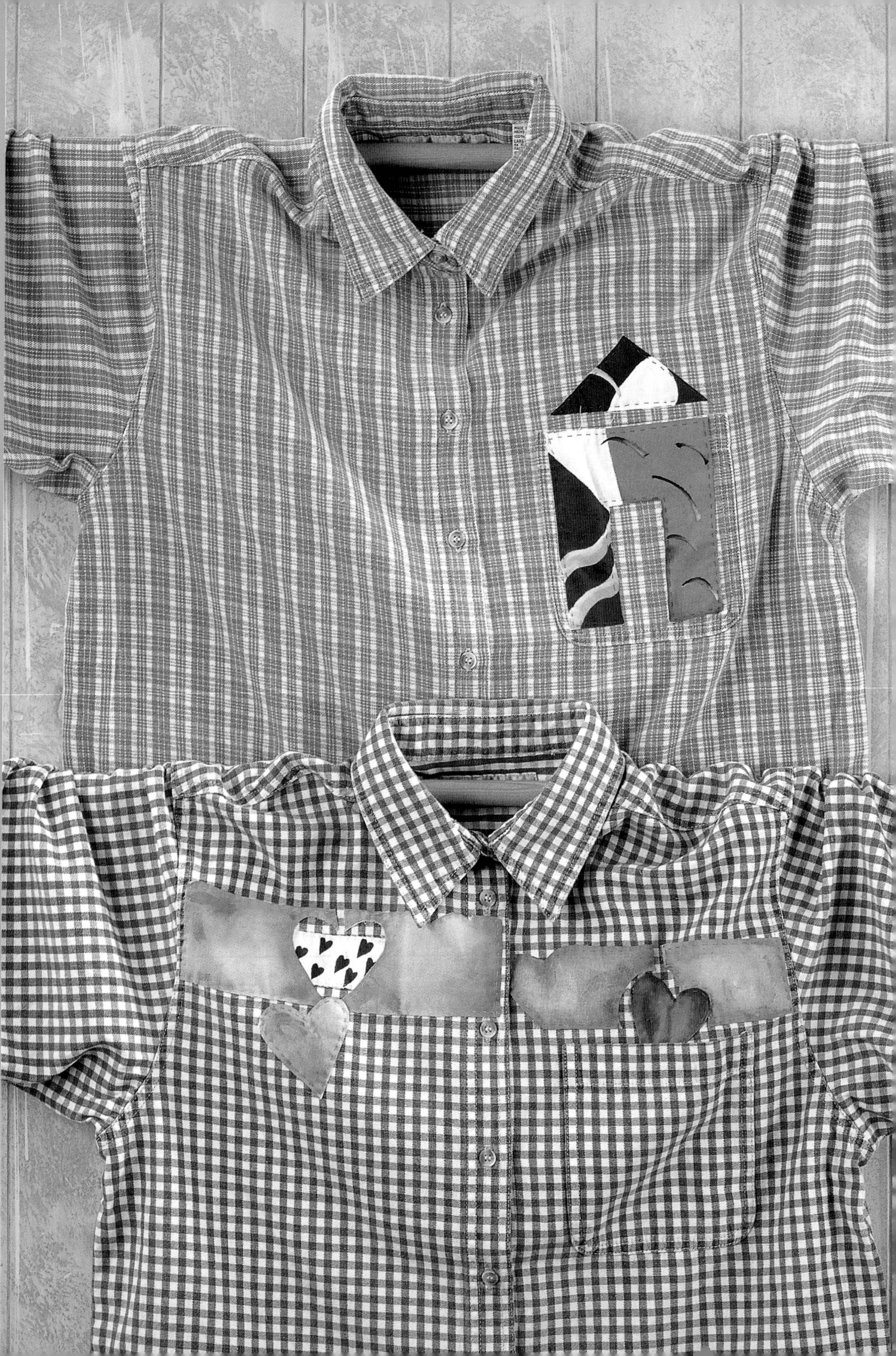

What you cannot find

on earth

is not worth seeking

Model Information

Row of Hears Pocket

Method: Mixed Media and Machine-Stitched
Enlargement: Actual Size
Fabrics: Cotton with Acrylic Paints mixed with Textile Medium (see page 21) and Ink

Wacky House Shirt

Method: Mixed Media and Hand-Stitched
Enlargement: 125%
Fabrics: Cotton with Acrylic Paints mixed with Textile Medium (see page 21)

Hidden Hearts Shirt

Method: Mixed Media and Hand-Stitched
Enlargement: 160%
Fabrics: Cotton with Acrylic Paints mixed with Textile Medium (see page 21)

Elegant Lace Shirt

Method: Mixed Media and Dimensional Ribbon Embroidery
Fabrics: Lace Motif; Burgundy, Blue, Green, Orange, and Terra-Cotta, 4mm silk ribbons

Row of Hearts Pocket Pattern

What you cannot find on earth is not worth seeking

Row of Hearts Pocket Pattern

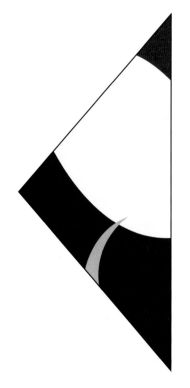

Wacky House Shirt Pattern

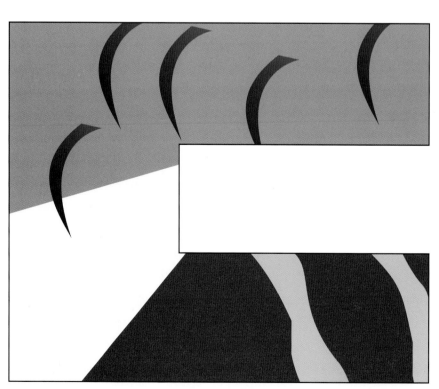

Hidden Hearts
Shirt Pattern

Elegant Lace
Shirt Pattern

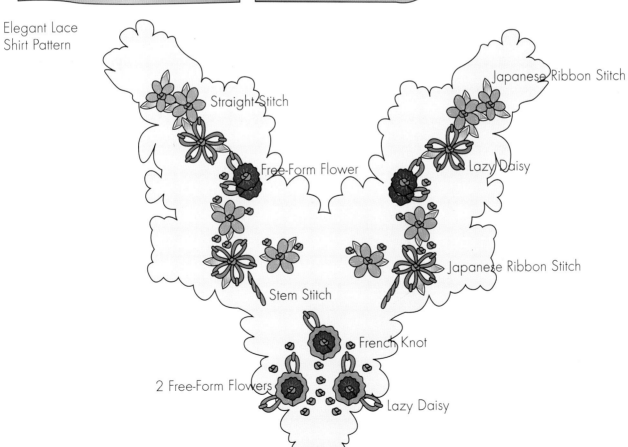

Japanese Ribbon Stitch

Straight Stitch

Free-Form Flower

Lazy Daisy

Japanese Ribbon Stitch

Stem Stitch

French Knot

2 Free-Form Flowers

Lazy Daisy

Model Information

Japanese Girl Pillow
Method: Mixed Media
Enlargement: 110%
Fabrics: Paper

Heart Stone Pillow
Method: Mixed Media and
  Hand-Stitched
Enlargement: 120%
Fabrics: Bronze-Colored Sculpting
  Medium

Pear Sachets
Method: Shadow Appliqué
Enlargement: Actual Size
Fabrics: Cotton and Sheer Rayon
*Note: Finishing instructions on
  page 106.*

Pieced-Rose Pillow
Method: Machine-Stitched
Enlargement: 170%
Fabrics: Cotton

Kimono Pillow
Method: Machine-Stitched
Enlargement: 165%
Fabrics: Screen-Printed Cotton
*Note: A ribbon sash and a pearl-
  ized fan button were stitched
  under sleeves.*

Japanese Girl Pillow Pattern

Pear Sachets Pattern

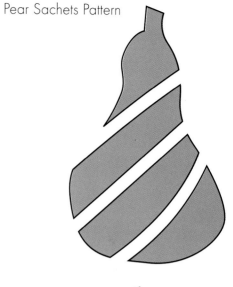

Heart Stone Pillow Pattern

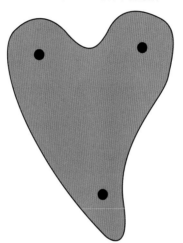

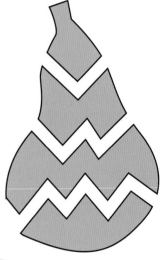

Kimono Pillow
Pattern

Pieced-Rose Pillow Pattern

You're the cat's

MEOW

• Pear Sachets •

Materials

¾ yd. of 1½"-wide ribbon
⅛ yd. sheer fabric; matching thread
5" x 5" piece of fabric for motif
5" x 5" piece of double-sided fusible web
Metallic thread
Potpourri

Instructions

1. Following manufacturer's instructions, adhere motif fabric to fusible web. Cut out motifs. Cut sheer fabric into three 3½" x 11½" pieces. Position motifs into place on one layer of sheer fabric and fuse, according to manufacturer's instructions. Layer one piece of sheer fabric on top of pear. Pin layers together. Hand-stitch edges of each section with metallic thread.

2. Cut two 11½" x 1½" pieces of ribbon. Sew ribbon along top and bottom of sachet. Sew remaining sheer fabric to bottom ribbon. Fold, right sides together, and sew last side of ribbon to sheer backing. Sew across one end. Turn and press. Fill loosely with potpourri. Sew end closed. Roll both ends under and tack in place.

• Contemporary Appliqué

Additional Designs

Additional Design

Model Information

Gold Ribbon Towel
Method: Dimensional Ribbon Appliqué
Ribbons: 1"-wide Gold Sheer, ⅝"-wide Gold Sheer,
   1"-wide Brown Ombré Wired, and Blue/Grey
   and Gold 4mm Silk

Spiral Flowers Towel
Method: Machine-Stitched (straight stitch along center
   of ribbon)
Ribbons: 7mm Rayon

Additional Design

Gold Ribbon Towel Diagram

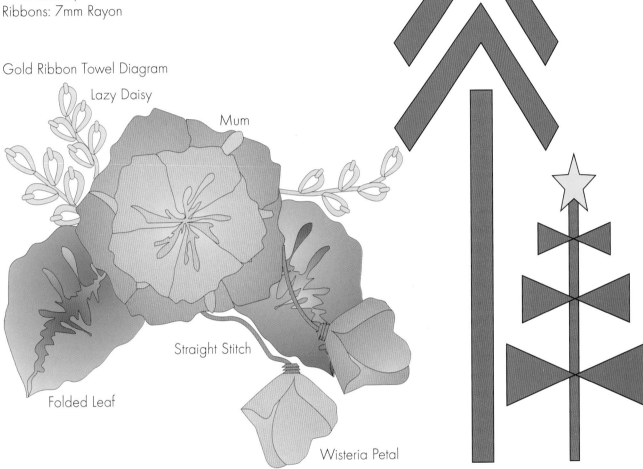

Lazy Daisy

Mum

Folded Leaf

Straight Stitch

Wisteria Petal

Spiral Flowers Towel Diagram

Model Information

Floppy Daisy Jumper

Method: Free-Standing Motifs, Machine-Stitched
Enlargement: 250%
Fabrics: Muslin and Cotton, and Denim Jumper

Floppy Daisy Jumper Pattern

Notes: Long strips of muslin were cut for daisy leaves and left to flop. Buttons were sewn to center of flower for texture.

Additional Designs

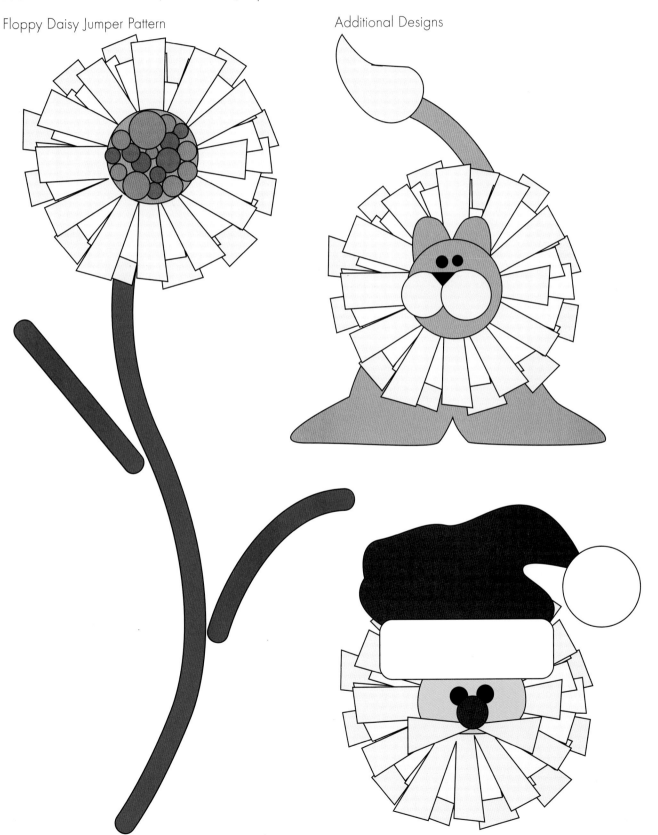

Flowerpot Apron
Method: Machine-Stitched
Enlargement: 245%
Fabrics: Polished Cottons

Flowerpot Apron Pattern

Additional Designs

• Daisy Jumper •

Materials

1 yard 60"-wide denim; matching thread
¼ yard muslin
2" x 45" torn strip of green cotton fabric; matching
    thread
2½"-diameter circle of tan fabric; matching thread
1 package of ½"-wide elastic
¾"-wide flat bias tape
15–20 old buttons

Instructions

1. From denim, cut two jumper straps 30" x 3½".
Cut two jumper ties 60" x 2". Cut one jumper piece
28" x 45".

2. Hem long edges of straps with a ¼" rolled hem,
top-stitching in place. Place a length of bias tape
down center on wrong side of each strap. Stitch
down both sides of bias tape to form casing. Thread
elastic through casing and stitch ends down.

3. Fold tie strips in half lengthwise and press. Fold
each edge in to center and press again. Topstitch
down both sides through all layers.
4. Lay jumper piece flat and mark center with a pin at
the top and bottom. Zigzag all edges of jumper. Fold
top edge down 2" and press. Repeat for bottom
edge.

5. Tear muslin into 1" strips and cut into 5" to 7"
lengths. Start flower in center of jumper about 6"
down from top. Layer muslin strips in a spoke fashion,
mixing lengths together. Pin tan fabric circle in center
and satin-stitch around edge. Sew buttons in center, allowing buttons to overlap. Tear green cotton fabric in
half lengthwise. Cut pieces desired length for stem
and leaves. Arrange on jumper, letting them twist and
curl. Sew a straight stitch down center of stem and
leaves. (See pattern on page 111.)

6. Mark and sew a buttonhole 3" up from bottom
edge of jumper in the center of front. Mark and sew
two buttonholes 3" down from top edge and 1¼" in
from side edges.

7. With right sides together, bring sides together and
sew up back seam. Sew the 2" hem in the top and
bottom. Stitch a casing in each hem at the 1" mark.
Thread ties through casings and out through buttonholes. Sew straps in place, adjusting for size desired.

• Flowerpot Apron Pocket •

Materials

½ yd. terra-cotton polished cotton; matching thread
Ruler or yardstick
Fabric-marking pencil

Instructions

1. Cut a 16½" x 15" piece of polished cotton. Fold
top edge down 3¾", wrong sides together. Press. Sew
¼" from raw edge
through both layers to
secure. Fold top edge
over 3" to right side to
form top of flowerpot.

2. Fold bottom edge up ½". Press.

3. Using ruler and
marking pencil, mark a
center line on the
wrong side of fabric. At
top edge, mark two ¼"
intervals out from cen-

ter. At bottom edge, mark ½" and ¾" out from center.
Draw a line connecting top and bottom marks. Fold at
lines to make box pleat. Bar-tack at top of pocket.

4. Mark ½" from bottom
left and right edges.
Mark a line from top
edges to bottom marks.

5. Cut along line. Fold
edges in ¾". Press. Pin
pocket in place on
apron. Sew along sides
and bottom. Tack at
center top. Fold in pleat
again and press.

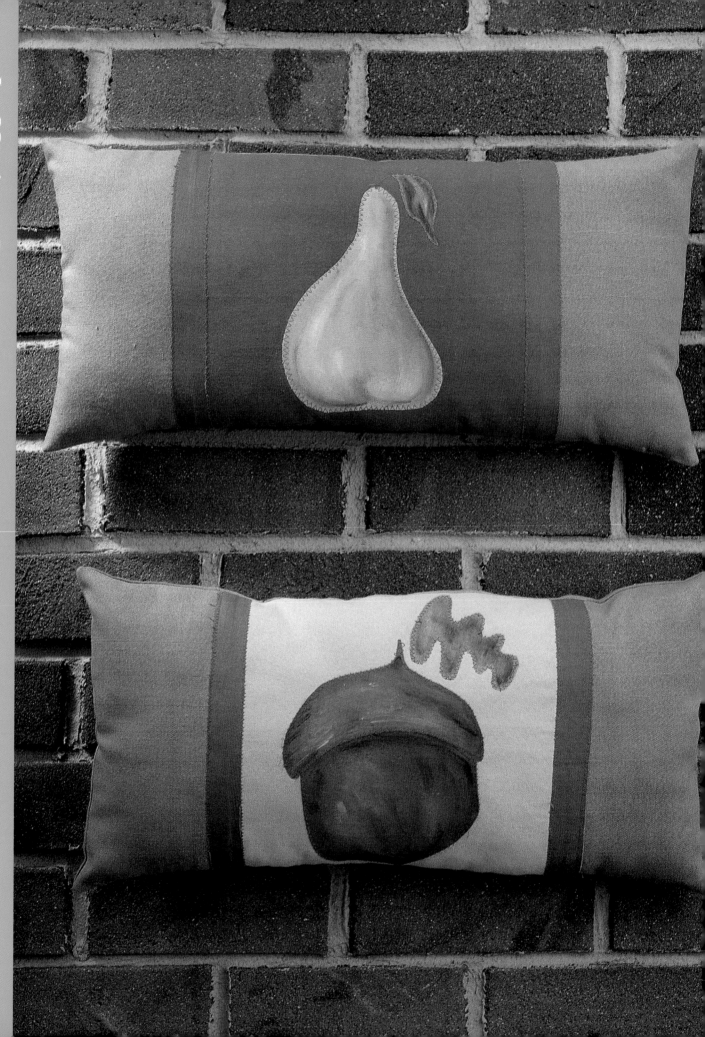

Model Information

Pear Pillow
Method: Machine-Stitched, Mixed Media
Enlargement: 155%
Fabrics: Cotton Twill

Pear Pillow Pattern

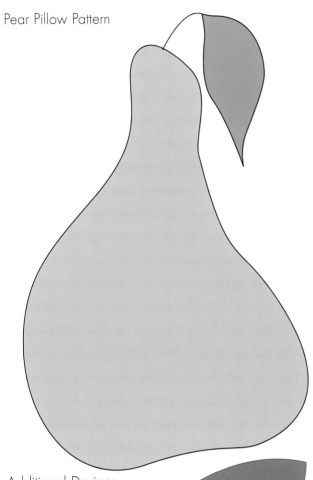

Acorn Pillow
Method: Machine-Stitched, Mixed Media
Enlargement: 220%
Fabrics: Cotton Twill

Acorn Pillow Pattern

Additional Designs

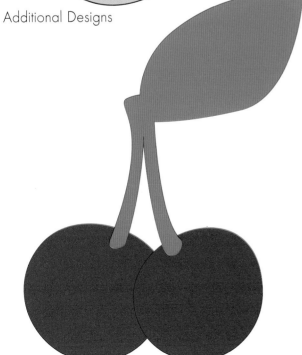

Model Information

Note: Black fine-tipped permanent fabric pens were used on all three projects.

Moon and Hearts Patches
Method: Hand-Stitched
Enlargement: 280%
Fabrics: Denims

What a Pair Patches
Method: Hand-Stitched
Enlargement: 200%
Fabrics: Cottons

Old Glory Patches
Method: Hand-Stitched
Enlargement: 150%
Fabrics: Polished Cottons

Moon and Hearts Patches Patterns

What a Pair Patches Patterns

Old Glory Patches Pattern

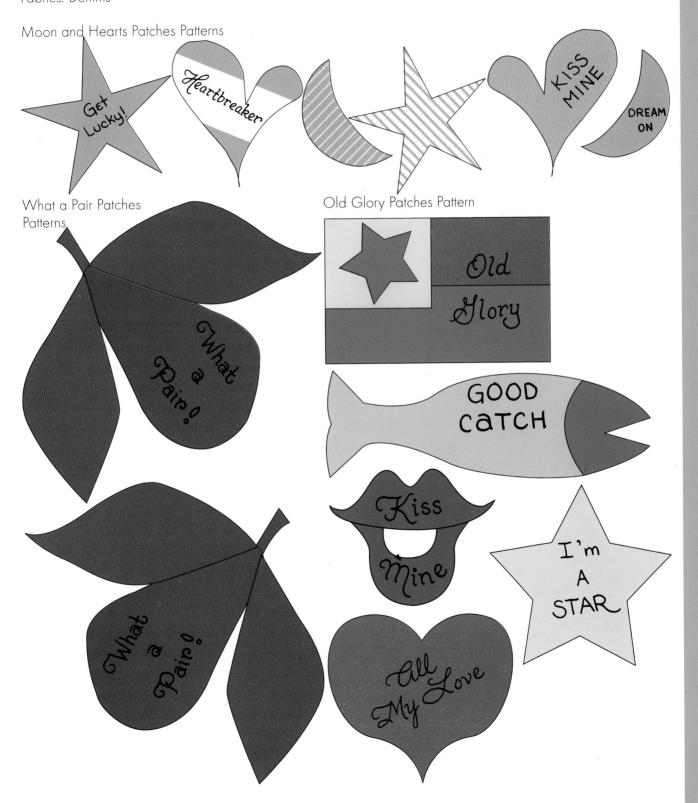

Model Information

Flowerpots
Method: Fused Appliqué
Enlargement: 135%
Fabrics: Cotton Calicos

Gardening Gloves
Method: Fused Appliqué
Enlargement: 180%
Fabrics: Printed Cottons

Flowerpots Patterns

Additional Designs

Sew the seeds of love!

Appliqué designs onto fabric or paper seed packets. Fill packets with seeds. Give the seed-filled packets to someone who needs extra love, joy, time, or hope.

Gardening Gloves Patterns

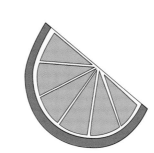

Model Information

Ivy Frame
Method: Dimensional Ribbon
Appliqué
Ribbons: 1"-wide Green Ombré
Wired, 7mm Pale Green Silk,
Green and Pale Green
Cotton Embroidery Floss,
and Couched Cording

Wisteria Lamp Shade
Method: Dimensional Ribbon
Appliqué
Ribbons: 1½"-wide Pale Blue
Sheer Chiffon, 9mm Light
Blue textured, 9mm off-white
textured

Violet Journal
Method: Dimensional Ribbon
Appliqué
Ribbons: ½"-wide Gold Sheer,
1"-wide Purple Cross-Dyed
Silk, 1"-wide Brown Ombré
Wired, and Dark and Light
Olive 4mm Silk

Fuchsia Umbrella
Method: Dimensional Ribbon
Appliqué
Ribbons: 1½"-wide Peach
Wired, ⅝"-wide Pale Green,
7mm Green Silk, and Grey,
Pink and Peach 4mm Silk

Layered Flower Derby
Method: Dimensional Ribbon
Appliqué
Ribbons: 1½"-wide Olive Wired,
1½"-wide Burgundy Ombré
Wired and 1½"-wide Striped
Burgundy Wired

Ivy Frame Diagram

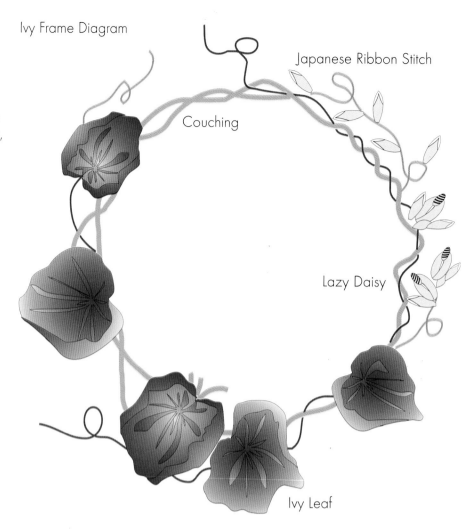

Japanese Ribbon Stitch

Couching

Lazy Daisy

Ivy Leaf

Wisteria Lamp Shade Diagram

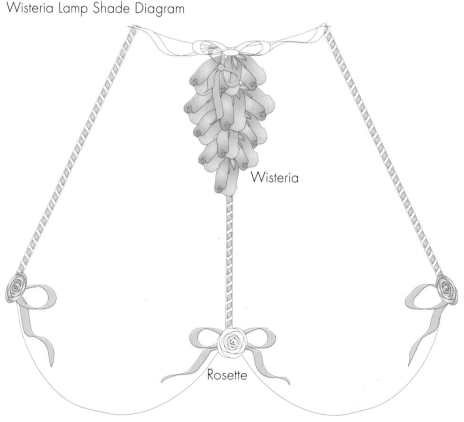

Wisteria

Rosette

Violet Journal Diagram

Violet

Ivy leaf

Straight Stitch

Fuchsia
Umbrella
Diagram

Lazy Daisy

Cascade

Fuchsia

Layered Flower
Derby Diagram

Layered Pointed-Petal Flower

Strawberries Tablecloth Diagram   Framed Daffodils Diagram

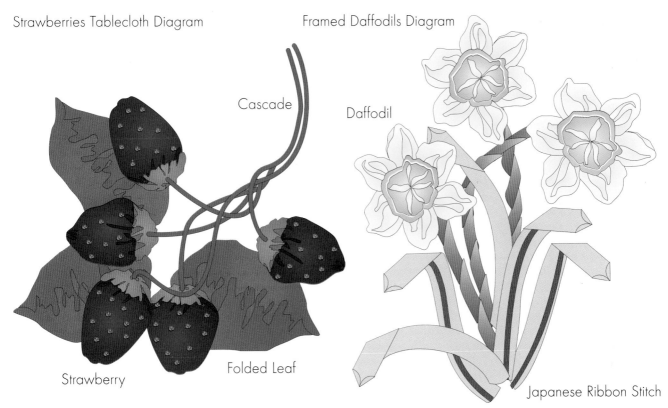

Cascade

Daffodil

Strawberry   Folded Leaf

Japanese Ribbon Stitch

Strawberries Tablecloth
Method: Dimensional Ribbon Appliqué
Ribbons: Two shades of 1½"-wide Red Wired, 1½"-
wide Green Wired, 7mm Olive Satin, and Green
Rattail Cording

Framed Daffodils
Method: Dimensional Ribbon Appliqué
Ribbons: 1½"-wide Yellow Ombré Wired, 1½"-wide
Green Ombré Wired, 7mm Green Bias Tape,
4mm Dark Olive Silk

• Ivy Frame •

Materials

Heavy cardboard (⅟₁₆" thick)
Lightweight cardboard (e.g., poster board)
1 yd. of white jacquard fabric
1 yd. of white homespun cotton
1 yd. ¼"-wide green and gold cording
Batting
Thin-bodied tacky glue
(See page 122 for ribbons.)

Instructions

1. From heavy cardboard, cut one frame, one back,
and one easel (see page 126 for patterns). From lightweight cardboard, cut one frame, one back, and one
easel. From jacquard fabric, cut one 4¼" x 8¼" piece

and two 8¼" squares. From homespun cotton, cut two
8¼" squares. Cut one frame from batting. Following diagram on page 122, appliqué ribbon, floss, and
cording to jacquard frame fabric.

2. Glue batting to heavy cardboard frame. Center
cardboard/batting frame, batting side down, on
wrong side of appliquéd jacquard frame fabric.
Pulling snugly, wrap and glue edges to wrong side.
Wrap and glue lightweight frame with homespun cotton frame fabric. Center and glue wrong sides of
frames together.

3. Wrap and glue heavy cardboard back with
jacquard back piece. Wrap and glue lightweight
cardboard back with homespun cotton. Center and
glue backs together.

4. Center and glue homespun sides of frame and
back together, leaving top open for picture. Glue
green and gold cording in between frame and back.

5. Wrap and glue heavy cardboard easel with 4¼" x
8¼" piece of jacquard, leaving top edge unwrapped.
Center and glue easels together with fabric extending
from top. Fold extending fabric over to back of easel.
Securely glue folded fabric to back of frame at top
dotted line. Glue a 3" piece of 1"-wide green ombré
wired ribbon between easel and back of frame at
dotted lines.

Enlarge patterns 225%.

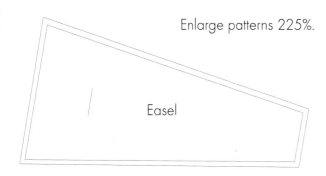

Easel

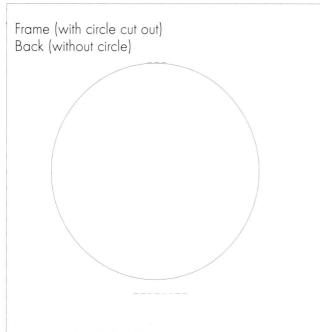

Frame (with circle cut out)
Back (without circle)

• Wisteria Lamp Shade •

Materials

Six-paneled small antique-looking lamp frame, scalloped at bottom
1½ yd. of ⅝"-wide off-white tatted trim
1½ yd. of ⅜"-wide off-white lace (weavable)
(See page 122 for ribbons.)

Instructions

1. Glue woven lace trim to outside of spokes. Glue ⅝"-wide tatted trim to top and bottom of lamp shade. Allow trim to extend over edge ⅛". Stitch six small mint-green bows to the base of each spoke. Drape tails on either side of scallop, knot end, and stitch in place. Stitch one rosette over each bow, alternating colors.

2. Arrange wisteria petals, following diagram on page 122, starting at the bottom. Stitch into place. Tie a bow with off-white 9mm ribbon, and stitch to uppermost part of wisteria, hiding raw edge of top petal. Swag tails and stitch to spokes on either side of cluster. Stitch remaining green bow to side of top petal.

• Fuchsia Umbrella •

Materials

Small wicker umbrella, flat on one side and scalloped at opening
11" x 7½" of mint-green fabric
12" x 9" of beige moiré
6"-diameter small ecru battenburg doily
Four 1½"-diameter white crocheted flowers
1 yd. of ⅝"-wide light olive wired ribbon
1 yd. each of pink, salmon, and grey/green 2mm silk ribbon
Tracing paper
Pencil
Hot glue gun and glue sticks
(See page 123 for ribbons.)

Instructions

1. Wrap tracing paper around umbrella, and make a pattern to fit umbrella. Leave about ½" finishing allowance (see example). Cut moiré fabric according to pattern, and appliqué design following diagram on page 123. Center appliquéd moiré on front of umbrella. Working quickly, hot-glue fabric to umbrella small portions at a time. Glue one raw edge down at center back. Fold top raw edge over ½". Overlap and glue onto back. Clip curves in front and hot-glue to inside pocket.

2. Wrap umbrella handle with ⅝"-wide light olive wired ribbon. Hot-glue in place at intervals, making sure to hide raw edges. Hot-glue crochet flowers in place at each scallop in front of umbrella.

3. Fold edges of mint-green fabric over ¼". Stitch in place. Hot-glue to inside pocket so that crocheted flowers are between green fabric and moiré.

4. Glue battenburg doily to back of umbrella. Fold and glue bottom loop on either side of the doily over to the front of umbrella. Cut a 9"-long piece of wired ribbon. Seam raw edges and gather-stitch one long edge. Pull gathers. Slip onto point of umbrella. Secure thread. Hot-glue in place. Tie three 2mm ribbons together in a bow. Hot-glue to the umbrella point just below the gathered ribbon. Swag ends and glue into place.

MM-Millimeters CM-Centimeters
inches to millimeters and centimeters

inches	mm	cm	inches	cm	inches	cm
⅛	3	0.3	9	22.9	30	76.2
¼	6	0.6	10	25.4	31	78.7
½	13	1.3	12	30.5	33	83.8
⅝	16	1.6	13	33.0	34	86.4
¾	19	1.9	14	35.6	35	88.9
⅞	22	2.2	15	38.1	36	91.4
1	25	2.5	16	40.6	37	94.0
1¼	32	3.2	17	43.2	38	96.5
1½	38	3.8	18	45.7	39	99.1
1¾	44	4.4	19	48.3	40	101.6
2	51	5.1	20	50.8	41	104.1
2½	64	6.4	21	53.3	42	106.7
3	76	7.6	22	55.9	43	109.2
3½	89	8.9	23	58.4	44	111.8
4	102	10.2	24	61.0	45	114.3
4½	114	11.4	25	63.5	46	116.8
5	127	12.7	26	66.0	47	119.4
6	152	15.2	27	68.6	48	121.9
7	178	17.8	28	71.1	49	124.5
8	203	20.3	29	73.7	50	127.0

yards to meters

yards	meters	yards	meters	yards	meters	yards	meters	yards	meters
⅛	0.11	2⅛	1.94	4⅛	3.77	6⅛	5.60	8⅛	7.43
¼	0.23	2¼	2.06	4¼	3.89	6¼	5.72	8¼	7.54
⅜	0.34	2⅜	2.17	4⅜	4.00	6⅜	5.83	8⅜	7.66
½	0.46	2½	2.29	4½	4.11	6½	5.94	8½	7.77
⅝	0.57	2⅝	2.40	4⅝	4.23	6⅝	6.06	8⅝	7.89
¾	0.69	2¾	2.51	4¾	4.34	6¾	6.17	8¾	8.00
⅞	0.80	2⅞	2.63	4⅞	4.46	6⅞	6.29	8⅞	8.12
1	0.91	3	2.74	5	4.57	7	6.40	9	8.23
1⅛	1.03	3⅛	2.86	5⅛	4.69	7⅛	6.52	9⅛	8.34
1¼	1.14	3¼	2.97	5¼	4.80	7¼	6.63	9¼	8.46
1⅜	1.26	3⅜	3.09	5⅜	4.91	7⅜	6.74	9⅜	8.57
1½	1.37	3½	3.20	5½	5.03	7½	6.86	9½	8.69
1⅝	1.49	3⅝	3.31	5⅝	5.14	7⅝	6.97	9⅝	8.80
1¾	1.60	3¾	3.43	5¾	5.26	7¾	7.09	9¾	8.92
1⅞	1.71	3⅞	3.54	5⅞	5.37	7⅞	7.20	9⅞	9.03
2	1.83	4	3.66	6	5.49	8	7.32	10	9.14